The Inner Rainbow

Paulist Press † New York/Ramsey

The Inner Rainbow

THE IMAGINATION IN CHRISTIAN LIFE

Kathleen R. Fischer

Acknowledgements

The Publisher gratefully acknowledges the use of the following materials: Excerpt from "Meditations of an Old Woman," copyright © 1955, 1956, 1957, 1958 by Theodore Roethke and © 1958 by Botteghe Oscure from the book, *The Collected Poems of Theodore Roethke*. Reprinted by permission of Doubleday and Company, Inc.; excerpts from *Four Quartets*, copyright © 1943 by T.S. Eliot; renewed 1971 by Esme Valerie Eliot, are reprinted by permission of Harcourt Brace Jovanovich, Inc. and Faber and Faber Ltd.; excerpts from *Markings* by Dag Hammarskjold, translated by Leif Sjoberg and W.H. Auden, copyright © 1974. Used by permission of Alfred A. Knopf, Inc.; excerpts from *The Poems of Gerard Manley Hopkins*, by Gerard Manley Hopkins, copyright © 1967 by The Society of Jesus. Used by permission of Oxford University Press, Inc.

Unless otherwise indicated, biblical quotations are from
The Jerusalem Bible, copyright © 1966
by Darton, Longman & Todd, Ltd., and Doubleday and Company, Inc.

Published by Paulist Press
545 Island Road
Ramsey, N.J. 07446

Printed and bound in the
United States of America

Contents

Preface

The rediscovery of the significance of the imagination for Christian faith is one of the most important events of our time. It is a struggle to return to a new and yet ancient way of experiencing and knowing, the way of myth and ritual, symbol and story, image and poetry. It is a struggle fueled by excitement, for we sense that freeing the imagination to live again could unlock new worlds and wonders for all Christians. In fact, this new interest in the imagination has already produced some remarkable metamorphoses.

Christians are again becoming a community of storytellers. A new look at the central role of story and poem in the Bible has helped us appreciate the importance of all forms of the language of the imagination—symbol, autobiography, poetry, and parable—as ways of expressing the mystery of God in human life. We have also learned that sharing our own story and hearing the stories of others is redemptive and healing. Through such telling we situate our stories within the larger narratives of our faith: the myth of Genesis, the story of the exodus of the Israelites from Egypt, the good news about Jesus Christ.

This revival of interest in the imagination is taking place within a new context of concern for the wholeness of human experience and knowledge, where reason and imagination need no longer be pitted against one another as rivals. Rather, we recognize the importance of the imagination in science as well as in art, religion, and poetry. A popular stereotype depicts a scientist as working exclusively with exact observations and logical reasoning. According to that stereotype, only statements verifiable by sense data are true. Such a stereotype forgets the role the imagination plays in all scientific knowing. Scientists employ metaphors and models as part of theory-construction and search for solutions to problems. And individual scientists like Albert Einstein acknowledge that awareness of the beauty and mystery of the universe is an important element in their scientific discoveries. The trip of the Voyager I spacecraft exemplifies our sense of the tentativeness of all efforts to know. As the spacecraft sped past the golden world of Saturn, providing a close view of the planet's rings, scientists were baffled. Photos of Saturn's numerous glistening rings revealed that at least two of the rings were braided together in a manner that defies explanation according to known laws. Scientists realized they were seeing things so remote from their experience that they had no hint as to their identity. Even in terms of science, we live in an age of awe and wonder, where mystery is a dimension of all knowing. In such a world, the imaginative language of symbol and metaphor is again recognized as an appropriate tool of thought.

Another front of renewal is research in the area of human physiology. Such research indicates that the two hemispheres of the brain control different functions. The right brain is responsible for the metaphorical, synthetic, and concrete; the left brain, for the linear, analytic, and rational. The right hemisphere of the brain seems to be more dominantly the source of those functions which we describe as imaginative, the aesthetic, mythic, and symbolic. Alerted by this information, many of us found that our right brains had atrophied from lack of use. Therapists realized the healing power of the right brain and began to employ image, fantasy, and metaphor as catalysts of healing and wholeness. Religious educators were reminded of the importance of right brain learning which occurs through art, dance, music, and liturgy. These were no longer regarded as educational fad and frill, but as essential to our entry into a deeper life of faith.

Developments such as the theology of story, recovery of the imaginative roots of science, and right brain research are evidence that a quiet revolution is building. Western civilization is gradually counterbalancing the mistrust of the imagination which has characterized our world since the Enlightenment. We are returning to what the philosopher Paul Ricoeur has called a "second naiveté." A "first naiveté," the unquestioning dwelling in a world of symbol, myth, and ritual, is probably no longer possible for us. But we can approximate such consciousness. The hope is that this revolution, this turn to the imagination, will open better ways of being for the human race and make human survival itself possible. For as awareness of the importance of the imagination has receded in our culture, we have relinquished human sensitivities and sources of power that can only be nourished by the imagination's language of story, ritual, art, and poetry.

This is especially true in the life of Christian faith. As the following chapters will try to show, the imagination is indispensable for a living faith. Our imaginations must be attentive if we are to hear the word of God, for that word is spoken primarily in symbol and story. This is also the level on which we make our initial response to the word of God heard in human life. The power of the imagination needs to be recovered above all in the daily life of Christians, in our reading of Scripture, our attempts to pray, our efforts to make moral decisions. Such are the areas, therefore, that this book addresses. By exploring the significance of the imagination for Christian faith, we hope to deepen our relationship to the Mystery at the center of human life.

I. Faith and the Imagination

The link between Christian faith and the imagination may seem tenuous at first. We associate faith with trust and commitment, and we trust or commit ourselves only to something that is real and reliable, worthy of our self-investment. These are not the traits popularly associated with the imagination. What does the imagination have to do with the real? Many of us, while not formally mistrusting the imagination, are at least vaguely uncomfortable with suggestions that it is essential to a life of faith. Why is this?

One source of mistrust is our fear that the world of the imagination is one of illusion and unreality. "I live in the real world," we say. Or, "Give me the facts." Such statements reflect a desire for the truth of clear ideas and empirical data. We associate the imagination with emotion and intuition, and we in the West are schooled to regard these as sources of error and deception. Neo-Freudians, for example, fail to distinguish imagination from hallucination in any definite way. In popular speech we often use the terms "imagination" and "imagine" to refer to subjective and unreliable experiences of reality: "It's just your imagination," we say. Or, "You must have imagined it." Our popular understanding of one imaginative form, "myth," is a tale that is unscientific and without foundation. No wonder, then, that bringing imagination into the discussion of faith appears to weaken faith's truth value and reliability.

Our personal uneasiness reflects a more widespread cultural discomfort with the role of the imagination. The respected writer of fantasy and science fiction, Ursula LeGuin, probes the American mistrust of the imagination in an essay entitled, "Why Are Americans Afraid of Dragons?"[1] Her diagnosis of this American malaise finds it rooted in America's value system. The imagination is a source of enjoyment and pleasure, the force behind fairy tales, art, music, dance, fiction, and poetry. Such enjoyment brings no immediate tangible profit, and therefore has no justification in a value system dominated by Puritanism, a work ethic, and the profit motive. It may even be dangerous and sinful. Our sexual biases also influence our attitude toward the imagination. American culture has described imagination as a feminine trait, since it is concrete, intuitive and emotion-laden in contrast to traditional masculine characteristics of reason and objectivity. LeGuin believes that our culture has thereby forced American men to establish their maleness by rejecting the essential human quality of the imagination. When we act out of such prejudices, our powers of imagination atrophy, and then we fear we have no imagination at all. Through such impoverishment of our personal and cultural imagination, we lose contact with important dimensions of reality.

Fortunately, we are gradually moving beyond the misconceptions and fears which have kept us from the riches that a fuller life of the imagination can bring. We realize that, far from endangering faith, the imagination evokes and nurtures it; revelation occurs first on the level of the imagination and so does our initial response of faith to revelation. The imagination, properly understood, provides access to the deepest levels of truth and allows us to live in the "real world." This chapter will show how this is the case.

A central image unifies our reflections on the meaning of the imagination and its relationship to faith: the imagination as inner rainbow. As sunlight is reflected and refracted by a curtain of falling rain, it produces a bow or arc of prismatic colors—red, blue, green, yellow—a rainbow. The rainbow is a universal and potent symbol. In the mythologies of many peoples the rainbow is a bridge linking heaven to earth; in Hopi and other Pueblo Indian myths, the Cloud People, who are the Sun and Earth's means of communicating with one another and humankind, travel on the rainbows. The brilliant colors of the rainbow have meaning to many peoples; some speak of living in the rainbow. A rainbow appears in the sky after the flood in Genesis, as sign of God's covenant with the earth and promise of a new world order.

> God said, "Here is the sign of the Covenant I make between myself and you and every living creature with you for all generations: I set my bow in the clouds and it shall be a sign of the Covenant between me and the earth" (Gen 9:12–14).

The rainbow signifies the divine presence, hope, reconciliation and rebirth. It often appears after a storm, an arc of color against a backdrop of clouds, a symbol of hope and promise.

The imagination is our inner rainbow in several ways. It is the bridge which joins God and the earth, the sacred and the secular, bringing them into unity in our life. The imagination enables us to live in multi-leveled, multi-colored truth, and to receive the truth which is pervaded by mist and mystery. It is also the human power that opens us to possibility and promise, the not-yet of the future. In all these ways, the imagination is essential to Christian faith. In what follows, we look more closely at these links between faith and the inner rainbow: (1) The Inner Rainbow as Bridge: Finding the Depth in the Ordinary; (2) The Imagination: Living in a Rainbow of Truth; (3) The Bow in the Clouds: The Imagination and Possibility.

The Inner Rainbow as Bridge:
Finding the Depth in the Ordinary

The Incarnation grounds the meaning and importance of the imagination in Christian life, for the Incarnation is God's entry into the details of human existence. Faith in the Incarnation is belief that the particulars of life are vessels of grace. Christian faith is not the turning to a God outside of this world; it is, rather, a relationship with a God who in Jesus Christ has chosen to become immersed in this world. Faith is a vision of life in which the entire order of things is sacred. As Karl Rahner states, in the light of Christian faith "the very commonness of everyday things harbors the eternal marvel and silent mystery of God and his grace."[2] The divine is the mystery which pervades and encompasses human existence, the grace and foundation of our life. Faith, then, is a gift which sustains a radical trust that this life, with all of its tears and laughter, its joys and sorrows, its loves and hates, its war and peace, is really worth living. Christian faith bids us say Yes to life in its concreteness: personal decisions, human relations, daily events, even death.

The imagination opens us to this experience of the Ultimate coming through finite reality, to the Depth at the heart of matter. For it is the imagination which knows the concrete in terms of its pervasive mystery. William Lynch, who has laid a foundation for a theology of the imagination in many of his writings, roots his discussion of its meaning in the fact that the imagination takes us through the finite to something more than finitude; finally, it takes us to God.

No matter what form the vision takes, however, or what its final goal—whether that be beauty, or insight, or peace, or tranquillity, or God—the heart, substance, and center of the human imagination, as of human life, must lie in the particular and limited image or thing.[3]

Lynch's emphasis on the importance of the imagination stems from his Christology. In Christ the conflict between the concrete and the unlimited is resolved. Christian faith is endangered if we withdraw from the things of the earth into a Platonic world of ideas and forms; it is also endangered if we see only the finite realities themselves, living our lives on the surface of Mystery.

The contemporary fiction writer, Walker Percy, sees the modern dilemma as just such a split between matter and spirit, a Cartesian dualism that results in the experience of a divided self. Under the influence of scientific theorizing, persons fail to experience the mystery of things. When matter and spirit are split asunder, everydayness is no longer a vessel of mystery; it is a source of ennui, discouragement, boredom. Percy describes the modern dread of everydayness in his article, "Bourbon."

> A man comes home from work every day at five–thirty to the exurbs of Montclair or Memphis and there is the grass growing and the little family looking not quite at him but just past the side of his head, and there's Cronkite on the tube and the smell of pot roast in the living room, and inside the house and outside in the pretty exurb has settled the noxious particles and the sadness of the old dying Western world, and him thinking: Jesus, is this it? Listening to Cronkite and the grass growing?[4]

Such boredom reflects the limits of scientific materialism, its inability to find mystery, transcendence, or presence within our culture. This makes a life of the spirit impossible. When the stuff of daily life ceases to point beyond itself, we have lost the occasion for the only encounter with the holy possible to humankind.

Concern over the kind of flatness of existence which Percy describes surfaced among Christian thinkers in the 1960's. Clustered around the question "Is God dead?" were discussions of our language about God, the relationship between the secular and the sacred, and the eclipse of mystery in human life. "Is faith obsolete?" some wondered. In the 1970's these questions regarding the possibility of faith for contemporary Christians led to a search for signals and experiences of transcendence within the human. This quest has led to awareness of the importance of the imagination as the human capacity which receives and responds to God's revelation in human life. When faith is seen primarily as the knowing of abstract truths rather than the readiness to see and hear God in the concrete, we may know some things about God, and yet never know God.

The imagination is fundamental to Christian faith because it is the inner rainbow which spans the difference between matter and spirit, holding them together in one act of experience and knowledge. In *The Rediscovery of Meaning, and Other Essays,* Owen Barfield describes this as the great discovery made by the poets and philosophers of the Romantic Movement. They realized that it is imagination which bridges the gap between matter and spirit; it is "a rainbow spanning the two precipices and linking them harmoniously together."[5] It is on the level of the imagination that we first encounter the divine in this world, for revelation is always given through the material; it is always symbolic, pointing to the ultimate through the finite. It is also on the level of the imagination that we formulate our initial response to the encounter with the divine; faith finds expression first as myth and ritual, sacrament, symbol, image and story. Only later does it become dogma and institution. It will be helpful to explore further how this is so.

When we reflect for a moment on our experience of knowing the world we find that there is one level on which we deal in ideas and concepts. We speak of qualities that characterize trees, or events, or human persons: they are beautiful, powerful, trustworthy. On this level we also speak of the religious beliefs we hold in faith: "God is the supreme being." Such an abstract level of knowing and speaking is important to all areas of human life. It is manageable and clear; it allows us to understand and exchange information. It is the source of theology and religious doctrine. But it is not the first and deepest level on which we know. There is a way of perceiving reality which includes concepts and information, but more than these; it also encompasses the concrete daily details of our existence. We perceive reality in terms of its concreteness through the power of the imagination. The imagination knows things in their individual uniqueness. It leads us not to the essence of trees or persons or emotions, but to *this* weeping willow in the autumn sunshine, to Alexis Zorba dancing on the shores of Crete, to *this* moment of terror in the face of capital punishment. Consequently, the imagination makes it impossible for us to bypass this world. We speak of the memories, relationships, or commitments of our lives. These are abstractions. When they actually occur, they meet us in vivid and individual colors: in our loss of this particular person, our relationship with this special friend, our time in this particular school. It is on the concrete level of existence that we have the strongest experiences of the interlacing relationships of our lives and the Mystery that creates and sustains us.

A moving embodiment of this reverence for the particulars of existence is found in the hero of Nikos Kazantzakis' novel *Zorba the Greek*. Alexis Zorba stands continually in amazement before those individual realities we have grown so accustomed to that we pass them by indifferently. Zorba marvels at the mystery of a woman, a man, a blossoming tree, a glass of cold water, seeing them every day as though for the first time. Zorba's wonder at the miracle of existence has a profound effect on his friend, the narrator of the novel:

> I felt, as I listened to Zorba, that the world was recovering its pristine freshness. All the dulled daily things regained the brightness they had in the beginning, when we came out of the hands of God. Water, women, the stars, bread, returned to their mysterious, primitive origin and the divine whirlwind burst once more upon the air.[6]

Zorba's vision of the ordinary calms the spirit, enlarges the heart, and creates joy.

Often we learn to love the particulars of existence only when we realize that we may be about to lose them. May Sarton's novel, *A Reckoning,* opens with such a realization on the part of its main character, Laura Spelman. Laura has just emerged from an interview with her physician, Dr. Goodwin, in which she has learned that she has inoperable cancer and has only a short time to live. With that news, she walks the two blocks down Marlboro Street in Boston to her car, aware how piercing in their beauty are "the low brick houses, the strong blue sky, the delicate shape of the leafless trees, even the dirty lumps of snow along the curb."[7] The challenge of a Christian spirituality is to live our present existence with this kind of appreciation of the unique and individual gifts of creation. It therefore requires an attentive imagination.

The paradox of the imagination is that, although it speaks in terms of individual and unique things, it always suggests more than it actually perceives and describes directly. Through the gift of the imagination we experience the tension between particular events and the mystery which they both reveal and conceal. Hence, the imagination speaks the language of transcendence. At times we experience this transcendence simply as the aura of mystery or a contact with inexpressible depths, as when we are part of a magnificent musical production or hear a moving piece of poetry. However, such experiences point to the One who is found in the depths and limits of our life. In faith we encounter the Mystery, the Transcendent, the Unknown within ordinary events. In *Belief Today*, Karl Rahner describes this capacity of the ordinary to reveal universal mystery. Faith reveals that these ordinary things "have unutterable depths, that they are indeed heralds of eternity, always vastly greater than they seem, like drops of water that mirror the immense vault of heaven."[8] It is the imagination which grasps the realities of our world in terms of their dimension of depth. As the inner rainbow, it brings together the sacred and the secular, allowing us to meet them in one event.

The Imagination: Living in a Rainbow of Truth

Faith and the imagination are linked in a second way; both approach truth in terms of the total person. Faith involves not reason or emotion or will alone, but the total being of a person. Faith is, as Paul Tillich has said, "an act of the total personality. It happens in the center of the personal life and includes all its elements."[9] Through faith we participate with our whole being in what Tillich describes as our ultimate concern, that which is of ultimate meaning and significance in our life. Christian faith, then, is more than a mental assent to propositions; it is the central relationship which affects our vision of reality. It leads to commitment and action. Love and action are implied in faith, and they cannot be separated from it.

The truth of the imagination is this kind of truth. The imagination involves the total person, on many levels, and calls for participation. A traditional saying by an unknown author sums up this sort of truth: "We live in a rainbow, not a pure white light of truth." Since the eighteenth century, which has been called the "Age of Reason," or the "Enlightenment," we have given priority to the truth of clear and distinct ideas. This ideal of clear-sightedness was based on mathematical and empirical methods for observing and understanding the world. However, not all kinds of truth can be captured with such clarity and detachment. The nineteenth century poet John Keats was one of those who feared that scientific reason was the enemy of poetry. Believing that Isaac Newton had destroyed all the poetry of the rainbow by analyzing its prismatic colors, Keats lamented in his poem *Lamia* that cold philosophy could "unweave a rainbow."

In *The Burning Fountain: A Study in the Language of Symbolism,* Philip Wheelwright approaches this question of truth in terms of two kinds of language. He distinguishes between expressive language, the language of symbolism, and steno-language, or the language of logical purity, reminding us, however, that the difference is not a dualism, since they differ in degree rather than kind. What Wheelwright calls expressive language is what we are calling the truth of the full rainbow. Steno-language is necessary for those human transactions where we must convey information in univocal and unambiguous ways, but it is not the only language of truth. There are truths of play, healing, surprise, confusion, and warmth in life which elude the confines of strict definition. We all have experiences which are too intense and deep to be captured in any language other than that of the imagination. One of the most universal of these experiences is love. Expressive language is the language of depth meanings. It arises within that area of human experience which is not available to logical or empirical verification; like a rainbow, it "pierces into the depths of the heart, and mounts upward to the dwellings of the gods."[10] Through such language we respond to and communicate our experience of the world which transcends finite existence but grounds and gives meaning to it.

We have all had experience of these two kinds of language and the kinds of truth they convey. An evening TV news broadcast brings home the contrast clearly. Although the presentation of the news may include film clips and other visual images, an attempt is made to convey the day's news to us in direct statements that are clear and logical, understandable by widely different audiences who are interested in economic situations, world events, and the activities of important figures. As the news breaks for commercials, we encounter another kind of communication. This is the language of advertising, the work of the "image industry." Through visual and sound images we are coaxed to associate designer jeans with beautiful bodies and sexual attractiveness, cars with chic style and financial power, perfume with romance and pleasure. The whole person is affected by this kind of language, often in ways we would be unable clearly to describe. Its effects will outlast the news.

Such advertising also illustrates the fact that the truth of the imagination is indirect. This indirectness of imaginative truth requires what Philip Wheelwright terms the "soft focus" of poetic language.[11] Wheelwright draws his metaphor from the field of photography, where, he says, the quality of the landscape can at times be most truthfully revealed through a blurring of its hard outlines. We have an experience of this kind of truth when we listen to a story, a symphony, or a poem. The truth does not reach us directly; it approaches from all sides. A story is told of Albert Einstein which illustrates this point. Einstein was once asked to describe the theory of relativity in simple enough language that the listener might capture something of its meaning. Einstein replied: "I cannot do what you request, but if you will call on me at Princeton, I will play it for you on my violin."[12] The theory of relativity had for Einstein a depth and range of mystery which it was impossible to convey in the kind of clear and direct answer the listener was seeking.

The language of Christian faith too conveys truth which is filled with depth and mystery. The process theologian Bernard Meland describes the structure of Christian faith as symphonic rather than logical. Faith's minor themes contain an implicit logic, but the overall movement of faith presents

> a dissonant situation in which contraries are simultaneously acknowledged and disavowed, in which resolution and peace are somehow attained, but not without the price of conflict, pain, and suffering; and not without a sense of taking into oneself, of bearing the burden of that over which one has triumphed.[13]

Revelation in this life is neither clear nor exact. As T. S. Eliot says in "The Dry Salvages", "the hint half guessed, the gift half understood, is Incarnation."[14] In succeeding chapters we will see how the truth of revelation comes to us in such indirect and multi-leveled ways, through the parables of Jesus, the images of the psalms, the poetry of Israel's prophets, and the paradox of such Gospel sayings as that if we want to save our life we must lose it.

The attempt to hold meaning and mystery together, to move from what we know to the less known or unknown, makes all language of the imagination basically metaphorical. Metaphor enables us to hold in tension what is concrete and graspable and what is vague and mysterious; it works simultaneously on all levels. The term we usually use for our first level of imaginative perception is image. An image arises from our emotional impressions of a particular event. It is an experience of embodied truth. We form an image of an ocean scene, a winter day, a gathering of friends around a supper table, a bird in flight, a freshly blooming rose. Frequently, as is the case throughout this book, the terms image and symbol are used interchangeably; there is no agreed upon distinction between them. However, one helpful way to distinguish image and symbol has been suggested. A symbol is a kind of image, but it is an image that has become more general, conventional, and permanent. Water, bread and wine, a rose, the swan are symbols. They have greater stability than many individual images and endure beyond a few occasions.[15] When a symbol becomes universal in the human psyche and has rich meaning for humankind in general, we speak of it as archetypal; the Great Mother and the river of life are examples of archetypal symbols.

The power of the imagination to hold multiple dimensions of truth in unity relies on analogy, a style of language and thought which illumines the meaning of one thing by reference to another. Isaiah says of the servant of the Lord:

> Like a sapling he grew up in front of us,
> like a root in arid ground (53:2).

Christian faith has always relied on analogy. William Lynch calls it "that habit of perception which sees that different levels of being are also somehow one and can therefore be associated in the same image, in the same and single act of perception."[16] The obvious and literal meaning of such language points to another meaning which is given within it. We cannot stand outside an image and decide how an image is like an object and how it is different. This is because there is an interpenetration of the sameness and the difference, the literal and fuller meanings, which makes total separation impossible. Lynch finds the mystery of this identity of sameness and difference most fully expressed in Christ, and finds in Christology the model for every analogical act of the imagination.

> It is no small wonder that it is in Christ we come to the
> fullest possible understanding of what analogy means in
> the fullest concrete, the facing relentlessly into the two
> poles of the same and the different, and the interpenetrat-
> ing reconciliation of the two contraries.[17]

The power of analogy is such that we cannot throw away the
metaphor or symbol after we have seen what it is pointing to.
Only by fully participating in the details of the symbol can we
experience the wholeness of the truth it conveys.

The truth of the imagination calls for participation. As
the American poet Wallace Stevens says, "we live in the
concepts of the imagination before the reason has established
them."[18] The truth of the imagination is embodied truth.
Because the imagination links us to the concrete, which is
where we live, it is experiential truth, and it cannot be had in
any other way. In *Unfinished Man and the Imagination,* Ray L.
Hart points out that, while all knowing exists in relationship to
events, imagination lives in closest proximity to them.[19] Since
reason puts us at a distance from events, its way of knowing is
clear, manageable, and free from strong feeling tones. We say
it is more abstract. Imagination, by taking us into the details of
the event itself, captures more of the emotion, ambiguity, and
intensity of it. The poet W. B. Yeats expresses this well in "A
Prayer for Old Age":

> God guard me from those thoughts men think
> In the mind alone,
> He that sings a lasting song
> Thinks in a marrow bone.[20]

To "think in a marrow bone" is to experience truth on the
many levels of the self which the imagination makes possible,
including emotional truth. Emotion may appear initially to be

a barrier to truth. Persons who get emotionally involved are thought less likely to see the truth than those who stand back and coolly analyze and organize information. However, as the philosopher Alfred North Whitehead has shown, it is in and through the emotional tone itself that we come to know the truth of events in their concrete totality. The fear and pain connected with a tragic death, for example, do not distract from its truth. They help us perceive the tragedy in its fullness. That is why the truth of the holocaust cannot be adequately conveyed in documents and statistics; the anguish and despair of the victims and their survivors are part of the truth and can often best be heard in fiction and poetry. Philip Wheelwright makes this point forcefully as it applies to poetic language. His thesis is that truly expressive symbolism awakens insight in and through the emotions it engenders; where an appropriate emotion is not aroused, full insight does not occur.[21]

Such participation in the truth of the imagination is able to transform us. That is one reason why it is essential to religious truth, whose finality is to convert us. Religious faith has always found expression first in such modes of participatory truth: ritual, symbol, myth, poetry, drama, story. The Australian Yuin tribe raises hands and weapons toward heaven in prayer. Miriam sings a paean of victory to celebrate God's deliverance of Israel. Early Christians gather for the breaking of the bread. In all these ways we see that imaginative truth is a dwelling place. What the poet Wallace Stevens says of hearing music illumines the way in which the imagination enables us to participate in its expressions of truth.

> When we hear the music of one of the great narrative musicians, as it tells its tale, it is like finding our way through the dark not by the aid of any sense but by an instinct which makes it possible for us to move quickly

when the music moves quickly, slowly when the music moves slowly. It is a speed that carries us on and through every winding, once more to the world outside the music at its conclusion. . . . When it is over, we are aware that we have had an experience very much like the story just as if we had participated in what took place.[22]

This ability to live the truth from within is especially important for understanding that difficult genre, the myth. One has to enter the world of the myth and participate in its concrete details to grasp its profound truth. Whether it be a myth of creation or fall, or myths of God or the gods, we cannot extract kernels of scientific and dogmatic truth and throw the story away. Demythologization is impoverishment. This is one of those areas where scientific and dogmatic statements are less adequate, not more adequate, to the truth than the language of imagination. No one was there when light came to be. No one ever saw God. No one even knows why the buzzard has no feathers on his head. When we tilt at the mystery here, we are trying to grasp the ungraspable, and a myth does it creatively, playfully, and with important dimensions of feeling, as we might best be able to experience by looking at a myth that is unfamiliar to us, the Cherokee version of "How the Sun Came."

There was no light anywhere, and the animal people stumbled around in the darkness. Whenever one bumped into another, he would say, "What we need in the world is light." And the other would reply, "Yes, indeed, light is what we badly need."

At last, the animals called a meeting, and gathered together as well as they could in the dark. The redheaded woodpecker said, "I have heard that over on the other side of the world there are people who have light."

The animals agree to send someone to these people to get light. First the possum goes, hoping to hide the light in his big bushy tail. But the sun is so hot it burns all the fur from his tail. Then the buzzard dives high over the place and catches a piece of the sun in his claws. He carries the sun home on his head, but it is so hot it burns off his head feathers, leaving the buzzard bald to this day. The animals are in despair, when Grandmother Spider speaks.

> "They have done the best a man can do," said a little voice from the grass, "but perhaps this is something a woman can do better than a man." . . .
> When Grandmother Spider came to the place of the sun people, she was so little and so quiet no one noticed her. She reached out gently, gently, and took a tiny bit of the sun, and placed it in her clay bowl. Then she went back along the thread that she had spun, with the sun's light growing and spreading before her, as she moved from east to west. And if you will notice, even today a spider's web is shaped like the sun's disk and its rays, and the spider will always spin her web in the morning, very early, before the sun is fully up. . . .[23]

Through myths such as this human beings try to describe why things are the way they are, what is meaningful in life, where life comes from, and where life is going. Such symbolic narratives link the sacred and the secular, grounding and giving meaning to human existence. We cannot live without myths; they are essential to our spiritual life. The myths by which we live may be disguised, but they are never eliminated. For the return and rebirth of myth we must look to the quality of our imaginations.

The imagination is essential to faith, then, because it enables us to live in a rainbow of truth, the kind of truth which affects the whole person, truth which embodies depth and mystery, and truth which calls for the kind of participation which is essential for personal transformation. In later chapters we will see how such an understanding of truth helps us incorporate the power of the imagination into our prayer, our process of Christian growth, and our moral decision making.

The Bow in the Clouds:
The Imagination and Possibility

The stories of Genesis which prepare for the account of Noah and the flood portray the deepening circle of sin which infects even the relationship between blood brothers in the story of Cain and Abel. Like a pebble thrown into a pond, producing ever widening waves, the first sin spreads. The ages of the patriarchs grow shorter and shorter; it is difficult to find any relationship not affected by the power of sin. Then the rainbow comes, to connect this world of sin and separation to the promise of God.

The story of the covenant which God makes with Noah draws us into a world of new possibility. It relates our immediate world of destruction, sin, and broken relationships with a not yet realized, but promised reality. The rainbow, the bow in the clouds, is the sign of this promise.

> God said, "When the bow is in the clouds I shall see it and call to mind the lasting Covenant between God and every living creature of every kind that is found on the earth" (Gen 9:16).

The rainbow is a symbol of redemption and hope, a sign that humanity will continue to exist. It is also a promise of a new order of relationships, reversing the broken and ruptured relationships between God and human beings, between person and person, and between humanity and the earth, which the preceding chapters of Genesis had woefully chronicled.

When we hear a word of hope, such as God's promise to Noah, we hear it first at the level of the imagination. The imagination then becomes the power which enables us to share in creating this promised future. It lets us envision what is not yet, what is still only possible. It grasps the Mystery which, while remaining mystery, lures us beyond our present actualities into ever new horizons.

Jesus' announcement of the kingdom of God works in this way. It presents possibilities for our present reality which we have not even entertained before: the blind seeing, the lame walking, the poor hearing the good news preached to them. Similarly, we must hear the proclamation of Jesus risen with our imaginations if we are to hear it fully. For the full meaning of that proclamation is that our present realities will be transformed in a promised future which lies outside our experience. Our efforts to share in bringing about the new order of relationships begun in Jesus' resurrection also require the life of the imagination for sustenance.

To understand the importance of the imagination to possibility, it is necessary to reflect on the connection between imagination and memory. At times the workings of the two are so intertwined as to be nearly indistinguishable. The unity of our inner life is such that many define imagination as the sum of our human powers as they focus on experience in its wholeness, enabling us to enter into concrete images of it.[24] The imagination loosens and dissolves past images in order to recombine them in new forms for the future. That is why the imagination can enliven our traditions. In Book XI of his *Confessions,* St. Augustine reflects on the meaning of time and describes how the imagination creates the present moment by fusing memories of the past with anticipation of the future. The imagination is not simply a passive or reproductive power, imitating the realities of our experienced world. It is a rainbow spanning the distance between past and future. From the world we know, we produce a vision of the world we want to build. The imagination uses the familiar to create the unfamiliar. Through the imagination a nation which has relied on war as a solution to conflict can see itself as a people turning swords into ploughshares and spears into pruning hooks. By means of the imagination, a persecutor of Christians like Saul can see himself as a witness to the Gospel of the cross and resurrection. This is the most widely recognized meaning of the imagination, the power which creatively envisions new possibilities.

Christian faith lives from hope, from the expectation of the promises of God. Since the imagination allows us to "see visions" and "dream dreams," it is a pentecostal power, enabling Christians to move forward in history. William Lynch, in *Images of Hope*, describes the imagination as the healer of hopelessness. Hopelessness is a sense of the impossible, a feeling of being trapped without options or alternatives. By contrast, the imagination shows a way out.

The imagination not only shows us a possible future; it evokes the energies needed to participate in the coming of that future. We often speak of a vision as firing or inflaming our imaginations. That fire or flame is a fuel which empowers our actions. By showing us new possibilities, the imagination releases and nurtures new energies. In the words of Roberto Assagioli, "Every image has in itself a motor-drive; images and mental pictures tend to produce the physical conditions and the external acts corresponding to them."[25] The Jesuit mystic and paleontologist Teilhard de Chardin understood this. His vision of point Omega is not just a picture of the future unity of all creation in Christ; the purpose of the symbol is to unleash the energy necessary to help create that future.

This sketch of the relationship between imagination and

possibility completes our initial reflections on faith and the imagination. We have seen how the imagination as our inner rainbow bridges the difference between the details of our ordinary life and their Depth or divine Mystery, how it is our avenue to the kind of truth central to faith, and how it supports the relationship between faith and hope. Through this general outline of the qualities of the imagination, we have caught some sense of the urgency of recovering the rainbow, of allowing the imagination to come to life again in Christian faith. We will deepen this sense of the importance of the imagination by showing how it can bring fresh approaches to several areas of Christian life: Scripture, spirituality, prayer, self-image, images of God, morality, and ministry.

Notes

1. *Literary Cavalcade* (February 1981), 41–43.

2. *Belief Today* (New York: Sheed and Ward, 1967), p. 14.

3. *Christ and Apollo: The Dimensions of the Literary Imagination* (New York: New American Library, 1963), pp. 20–21. For very helpful insights on faith and the imagination see also John Shea, *Stories of Faith* (Chicago: The Thomas More Press, 1980); Amos Niven Wilder, *Theopoetic. Theology and the Religious Imagination* (Philadelphia: Fortress Press, 1976).

4. *Esquire* (December 1975), 148.

5. (Middletown, Connecticut: Wesleyan University Press, 1977), p. 150. See also Lynn Ross-Bryant, *Imagination and the Life of the Spirit* (Chico, California: Scholars Press, 1981).

6. Trans. Carl Wildman (New York: Simon and Schuster, Inc., 1952), p. 51.

7. (New York: W. W. Norton & Company, 1978), p. 7.

8. P. 15.

9. *Dynamics of Faith* (New York: Harper & Row, 1957), p. 4.

10. (Bloomington: Indiana University Press, 1968), p. 3.

11. *The Burning Fountain*, pp. 86–87.

12. Recounted by Norma H. Thompson in "Art and the Religious Experience." In *Aesthetic Dimensions of Religious Education,* ed. Gloria Durka and Joanmarie Smith (New York: Paulist Press, 1979), p. 44.

13. *Fallible Forms and Symbols* (Philadelphia: Fortress Press, 1976), p. 75.

14. In *The Complete Poems and Plays. 1909–1950* (New York: Harcourt, Brace & World, 1952), p. 136.

15. See James Hillman, "An Inquiry into Image," *Spring* (1977), 62–88; and Philip Wheelwright, *Metaphor and Reality* (Bloomington: Indiana University Press, 1962), pp. 92ff.

16. "Theology and the Imagination," *Thought* 29/112 (Spring 1954), p. 66.

17. *Christ and Apollo,* p. 158.

18. *The Necessary Angel, Essays on Reality and the Imagination* (New York: Vintage Books, 1951), p. 154.

19. (New York: Herder & Herder, 1968), p. 242.

20. *The Variorum Edition of the Poems of W. B. Yeats,* ed. Peter Allt and Russell K. Alspach (New York: The Macmillan Company, 1957), p. 553.

21. *The Burning Fountain,* p. 70.

22. *The Necessary Angel,* p. 126.

23. Alice Marriott and Carol K. Rachlin, *American Indian Mythology* (New York: Thomas Y. Crowell Company, 1968), pp. 30–32.

24. See William Lynch, *Images of Hope* (New York: New American Library, 1965), p. 209, and *The Necessary Angel,* p. 61.

25. *Psychosynthesis* (New York: Penguin Books, 1976), p. 144.

II. Imagination and Scripture

The first question we often ask of a passage in the Bible is: Did it really happen? Did three magi follow a star from the east to Bethlehem? Was Abraham a real person? Did the Israelites pass through waters to escape the pursuing Egyptians? We hope to discover that the events in the Bible are actual historical events. Then they are true. We can trust them as the basis of our faith. In addition, we can answer any challenges to the historical basis of that faith. Books and passages which do not readily fit this standard of verifiable historical truth—Jonah, Wisdom, Revelation, the infancy narratives in the Gospels of Matthew and Luke—are a source of confusion and doubt.

Yet somehow a lingering disappointment accompanies even our successes in substantiating the historicity of the Bible. We may understand the tribal structure of the Israelites, the prescriptions of the covenant code, and the circumstances behind the writing of the four Gospels. Yet we still wonder what all of this has to do with our life. Instead of bringing us closer to the Scriptures, such historical knowledge deepens our distance from the world of the Bible. What we really search for is the relevance of the biblical message to our own setting.

One way to bridge the historical distance, we are told, is to insert ourselves into the world of the Bible. Learn to think like a Hebrew. Find out what the author of the Book of Genesis really intended to say. Try to hear the message of Paul as it must have been received by the first Christians. Since the biblical writers lived in other cultures and centuries, biblical exegetes attempt to take us back three thousand years or so to the writers' time. We soon find, however, that such a leap out of our historical context is neither possible nor profitable. It is hard to find a way back to our own world. We continue to wonder what these past events have to do with our present concerns. What we thirst for is the power of God's word in our contemporary lives.

Now a change is taking place in biblical criticism which promises to unlock more of the power of the Scriptures for us. A new interest in the literary qualities of the Bible now accompanies attention to the Bible as history. Historical criticism, the biblical science that helps us answer questions about the original setting of a biblical book, its authorship, or the customs and terms it mentions, remains an important aid in reading the Bible. However, exegetes are showing a keen interest in the kinds of language through which biblical truth is conveyed to us. The goal is to allow the words, images, and stories of the Bible to make their full imaginative and emotional impact on us. Biblical scholars such as Amos Wilder have noted: "*How* Jesus and his followers spoke and wrote could not be separated from what they communicated."[1]

Not only must we pay closer attention to the revival of the imagination in reading Scripture. We must begin with the imagination. Attention to historical questions of authorship, the development of texts, and the origin of customs is not the starting point. Rather, historical knowledge supplements and supports our initial entry into the symbol and poetry of the biblical text. This chapter shows how important the imagination is in an effective encounter with Scripture. It does so in terms of two questions: *Why* begin with literary qualities rather than historical questions? *How* do we read the Bible in this way? To answer the question why, we look at the nature of revelation as symbolic disclosure. To answer the question how, we propose some guides for reading scriptural texts.

Revelation Through Symbol

When we preach from a biblical passage, read the Bible in study groups, or provide courses on the Bible as part of religious education programs, those who listen are interested in more than knowledge. They do want to know more about the Bible. But they look for the kind of understanding of the Scriptures which builds faith and inspires good works. In short, they desire a knowledge that carries also the power of God's word. Christians believe that the Bible *is* God's word. That is why we call it revelation. It is a sacred book which shapes personal and community identity. The way we interpret the Bible, then, depends on our understanding of the way in which God's revelation takes place. How does God's self-manifestation reach us?

There are many ways of understanding divine revelation. One is to view history as the supreme locus of divine communication. According to this view, Scripture presents a God whose self-revelation occurs through mighty deeds in history. The biblical scholar, Bernard W. Anderson, summarizes this view well in his popular introduction to *Understanding the Old Testament.*

From Israel's standpoint, this history is not just the ordinary story of wars, population movement, and cultural advance or decline. Rather, the unique dimension of these historical experiences is the disclosure of God's activity in events, the working out of his purpose in the career of Israel. It is this faith that transfigures Israel's history and gives the Bible its peculiar claim to be sacred scripture. To put it in a nutshell, the Old Testament is Israel's witness to its encounter with God.[2]

Historical deeds contain the action of God, but it is not always clear what God is doing. So God raises up inspired interpreters or prophets to explain the meaning of such events as the exodus and exile. This notion of revelation in history has been our customary way of understanding the nature of biblical revelation. It undergirds the idea that the Scriptures are a history of salvation, a history of God's saving action on behalf of a people. But problems arise if history is seen as the exclusive arena of God's revelation. We may begin to equate the truth of revelation with verifiable facts and events. Truth then becomes correspondence with external reality. If we ask of the biblical text only "Did it happen in this way?" we are liable to miss the truth. For truth is always embedded in a social and literary, as well as historical, context; facts alone do not create the truth. Important as it is, history by itself is not sufficient to account for all experiences of revelation.

Another understanding of revelation, one which appreciates historical events but places them within a broader context, is gaining importance today. It holds that God's revelation is disclosed in symbol. Or, as Avery Dulles phrases it, revelation "is mediated through symbol—that is to say, through an externally perceived sign that works mysteriously on the human consciousness so as to suggest more than it can clearly describe or define."[3] Although this understanding of revelation is expressed somewhat differently by thinkers such as Karl Rahner, Paul Tillich, Paul Ricoeur, and Ray L. Hart, its basic premise is that God's self-communication is always mediated to us through the experience of the world. How else can revelation reach us, since we ourselves are incarnate spirits who know the invisible only through its visible and material forms? For Christians, the incarnation is the fullest statement of this divine disclosure in a revelatory symbol. For this reason, Christian theology speaks of Christ as the sacrament of God: Jesus Christ is a symbol in the deepest and most primary sense, the grace of God visible and effective in our lives.

Since all of life is potentially sacramental, an infinite variety of symbols may mediate God's self-communication to us. The symbolic disclosures of revelation may be historical persons or events, such as the exodus of Israel from Egypt or the crucified and risen Jesus Christ. But revelation may also come through natural and cosmic objects or occurrences such as sun or wind. A burning bush, a sacred stone, the experience of forgiveness and reconciliation, or an artistic object—all these can be transparent to the divine. So, too, can words or writings: the poetry of Jeremiah, the myth of creation, the parables of Jesus. These linguistic symbols are the way we encounter the deeds of history as revelation. All forms of symbolic disclosure suggest more than they can clearly state, and lead us into the darkness where God dwells. They bring us meaning and at the same time preserve its context of mystery. Now, as we have seen, symbolic disclosure is the language of the imagination. If, then, revelation reaches us through symbol, it comes to us primarily on the level of the imagination.

In later sections of this book, we look at what this understanding of revelation means for the significance of art and ritual. Here our interest is primarily in how it affects our reading of Scripture. Symbolic language calls for participation. Symbols reveal truth by inviting us to enter in imaginatively. They evoke our entrance into worlds different from our own, and challenge us to new, sometimes even foreign, horizons. Nathan Mitchell describes this dimension of symbols nicely: "A symbol is not an object to be manipulated through mime and memory, but an environment to be inhabited. Symbols are places to live, breathing spaces that help us discover the possibilities that life offers."[4] Through the breaking of bread and drinking of wine in the Eucharist we enter into the meaning of Jesus' death for him and for us. We broaden our vision to the dimensions of Jesus' vision. We enter into redemption, liberation, covenant.

What Mitchell says of symbols generally is applied by Paul Ricoeur directly to the interpretation of biblical passages. To see a text as making sense for me is to see not just the history behind it, but also the world in front of it which opens for my commitment.[5] A symbol enables us to find ourselves in the new world of meaning or possibility which it discloses. So, viewing Scripture as symbolic disclosure means that the books and passages that we read are not only windows into the past, into the world of the author and first believers. These books and passages are also windows into the present and future, revealing new understandings of self and others, and disclosing new possibilities for discipleship.

Scripture contains images and patterns which light up other areas of experience. H. Richard Niebuhr refers to this as the paradigmatic quality of historical events and says that revelation might best be understood as an event that so captures a community's imagination that it alters that community's way of looking at all of experience.[6] The exodus, with its Sinai covenant, and the experience of the exile were for Israel such paradigms of human experience. It was not so much a question of what happened, but of what was always happening. The function of the paradigms was to illumine other areas of Israel's life, to provide a pattern for understanding her personal and communal joys and sorrows, failures and hopes. Exodus, the going out of Egypt, is the paradigm for liberation from other enslavements and alienations: want, fear, war. Israel's story is one of imprisonment and release, revealing that total and unreserved engagement with God is the way to final freedom. The covenant is also a paradigm. As Israel's prophets make clear, trampling on the poor and needy is a breach of their covenant with God. Likewise, the image of a new covenant shapes Israel's hopes for future salvation.

Symbol, like all imaginative language, has evocative power as well. It is able to involve all levels of the person, including emotions and will. The transforming power of any symbolism is rooted in this capacity to evoke and involve the total personality. Symbols get action. That is why all religious and political movements use extensive symbolism, whether it be the cross of Christians or the flag of the United States.

If God's revelation comes to us in symbol, and symbolic disclosure demands participation so that it can have its effect, we cannot stand outside the biblical text in the attitude of a scientific observer. Rather, as Amos Wilder has so aptly said,

> we appropriate the myth and symbol of the New Testa-
> ment by opening ourselves to its wisdom in the same order
> of response with which we encounter art or read poetry.
> Though this order of knowing is closer to that of ancient
> spell or visionary realization, or the world-making of the
> child, yet it is, for this very reason, a total and immediate
> kind of knowing and one that involves us totally.[7]

When a literary approach to the Bible is predominant, our interpreting is more an art than a science.

We must pay closer attention than before to the *form* in which the biblical message is presented, as an essential part of hearing the word. The past decade has highlighted the widespread use of imaginative language in the biblical writings, as well as the necessity of understanding how this language confronts a listener, causing him or her to identify with its message. The sections of the Hebrew Scriptures most quoted in the New Testament are poetry: the Psalms and the Book of

Isaiah. The forms most prevalent in the New Testament are the drama, the narrative, and the poem. As James Barr points out, even where a biblical story has an historical basis, it is the story as story that lives on and influences the life of the community.[8] That is why even people virtually ignorant about the Bible can tell the Christmas story. Narrative has provided a way of remembering. Jesus' message shows an imagination filled with the concrete images of daily life in Galilee: withering fig trees, fields of grain ready for harvest, sheep and shepherds. His teachings contain numerous examples of parables, paradox, and hyperbole which appeal directly for imaginative participation. This is what interests many exegetes now. William A. Beardslee explains in *Literary Criticism of the New Testament* that literary criticism has moved beyond questions of the authorship, date and sources of the biblical books to ask how the literary forms of the New Testament function.[9]

Convinced of the nature of revelation as symbolic disclosure and of the widespread use of imaginative forms for the biblical message, our question becomes a practical one. How do we allow such awareness to influence our actual reading of the Bible? How do we begin at the level of imaginative participation rather than that of scientific analysis? The next section suggests some ways in which renewed interest in the symbol and poetry of faith can affect our reading of Scripture.

Imagination and Scripture: Some Guidelines for Reading

Our concern in approaching Scripture in a new way is to take seriously the creative power of language and form. We want to live the biblical story so that it becomes our own story. Only then can the biblical word produce the same saving effect which it created in Israel and the early Church. To hear the Bible in this way we must learn to listen attentively. Elie

Wiesel in *Souls on Fire* describes how his grandfather taught him that "to listen is to receive." We do not force the text to submit to us; we receive it. Wiesel listened intently to his grandfather's Hasidic tales, and so was carried into a universe "where facts became subservient to imagination and beauty."[10]

We come to a biblical passage with contemplative openness to its word, and with awareness of the personal questions and concerns that have brought us there. In this spirit we (1) attend carefully to the text itself, (2) call on historical and literary criticism for assistance, and (3) celebrate and live the text within a community of faith. Let us explore each of these steps more closely.

1. *Attend Carefully to the Text Itself*

This may seem like strange advice. However, many Christians are afraid to trust their reading of a biblical text. We are aware that between us and the text stands the vast amount of learning that scholars have accumulated on the Bible over the years. We fear that we do not know enough to understand the Bible itself, so we turn first to a commentary or a theology book to help us find our way through it. Or our problem may be that a passage like Jesus' calming of the storm or the wedding feast at Cana seems all too familiar. It is so familiar, in fact, that we merely glance at it and assume that we know what it says.

However, the text is a locus of revelation. As revelation, it is not simply information; it is a relationship in which we are called to participate. We enter into a dialogue with the text, bringing our questions to it and allowing the biblical questions to address us: "Whom do you seek?" "Do you love me?" "Who do you say that I am?" The literary forms of the Bible can draw us into such a dialogue, since they are personal and searching. They can have this power, though, only if we really attend to the text and hear what is taking place in it.

One help in reading the text is to think of it as woven of

many threads, like a tapestry on a loom. These threads or elements that make up the texture of a biblical passage are the characters, their actions and interactions, the oppositions and contradictions that are woven into the text, and the beginning and ending which hold the passage together. An example will help to show how attention to the interrelated patterns and images within a biblical passage enables us to hear it in a fresh way and brings its power to life for us again.

The story of Jesus' meeting with Zacchaeus in Luke 19:1–10 needs to be read and reread attentively if we are to notice its detail and richness.[11] The two principal characters in the story are Jesus and Zacchaeus. In the first part of the story, this prophet who travels through Palestine teaching and healing is called simply "Jesus." He draws large crowds and attracts Zacchaeus' attention. Then something we may not have noted before occurs in the second part of the story: there is a change of names. In verses 7–10 this man Jesus is called "Lord" and "Son of Man," names of superior importance, suggesting divine titles. This change ties together the beginning and ending of the story. In verse 3 we are told that Zacchaeus "was anxious to see what kind of man Jesus was." He discovers that Jesus is Lord.

The passage presents the second character, Zacchaeus, to us in detailed fashion. Zacchaeus is rich, but his riches may not always have been acquired honestly, for he is called a sinner (7) and Zacchaeus himself wonders "if I have cheated anybody" (8). He is also a searcher, who cannot find what he is looking for: "He was anxious to see what kind of man Jesus was, but was too short and could not see him" (3). At the end of the story this searching is transformed: "salvation has come" (9); "the Son of Man has come to seek out and save" (10). Zacchaeus was looking but could not find; Jesus comes to save and brings salvation. The story also shows the transformations which take place in the actions of Zacchaeus through this experience. In the beginning he is one who takes in, who gathers taxes. At the end of the story he shares and gives to others. He welcomes Jesus into his home (6) and gives his goods to the poor (8).

As we hear the details of this story, it reaches out to involve us. Zacchaeus finds joy in giving up his previous actions. He finds the Lord in Jesus, and this involves a transformation of his life. We, too, are searching to find out who Jesus is. And we are also sinners in need of forgiveness. We bring to the passage many questions about Jesus and about our own lives. In the story of Zacchaeus we see that our search may transform not only our initial questions, but our very way of life. The story challenges us to be changed by the discovery of Jesus, to face our own need for repentance. In addition, it creates a yearning for the joy Zacchaeus found in such change. The horizon of the biblical text fuses with our own horizon, giving us a deeper understanding of what salvation means.

As we become more familiar with a particular book of the Bible, it is also helpful to read biblical passages in light of the whole book. For example, we read the story of Zacchaeus with care not only when we read the questions within the story, but also when we hear in it echoes of Luke's other narratives and sayings. This individual story reflects Luke's major concerns and themes: Jesus as Savior bringing universal salvation, Jesus' care for the poor and outcasts, his compassion and mercy, and his gift of messianic joy. The story of Zacchaeus expresses these themes of Luke's Gospel in summary form. Therefore, reading this passage in light of the whole Gospel provides a constant interplay between text and context.

The Books of Ruth, Genesis, and the Song of Songs provide further illustrations of this kind of reading. Opening the pages of the Book of Ruth, we may be struck first by Ruth's fidelity to her mother-in-law, captured in the familiar refrain of 1:16–17: "Wherever you go, I will go; wherever you live, I will live." The book is the story of Ruth, a Moabite woman who, after the death of her husband, refuses to leave her mother-in-law, Naomi. They travel together to Bethlehem, where Ruth weds Boaz, a relative of her husband, and gives birth to Obed, the grandfather of David.

Reading the Book of Ruth as if it were revelation for us in symbolic form, we feel its invitation to enter into the rhythm of emptiness and fullness which occurs not only in our relationship to the earth, but on the widest personal and social levels as well.[12] The opening verse of the book sounds this theme: "famine came to the land." This emptiness of the land is the setting for the loneliness of the widow which is described in verse 3: "Elimelech, Naomi's husband, died and she and her two sons, were left." Naomi's two sons, one of them Ruth's husband Chilion, also die. The force of emptiness is further felt in the contrast between the barrenness of an old woman and the fullness of bearing children in verses 11–13: "And Naomi said, 'You must return, my daughters; why come with me? Have I any more sons in my womb to make husbands for you? Return, my daughters; go, for I am too old now to marry again.' " These images of famine, loneliness, and barrenness bring to life our personal experiences of anguish and loss and our own feelings of uselessness and despair.

Over against this deepening sense of emptiness, the story introduces the symbol of plenty: Naomi and Ruth return to Bethlehem "at the beginning of the barley harvest" (22). This harvest image is the beginning of a movement of healing and the foreshadowing of a solution to Naomi's and Ruth's problems. The gathering of the harvest is the central image in the second part of the book.

> Everything culminates and merges in this image of ingathering: the wings of the Lord sweeping in to himself the people, the arms of Boaz gathering in to himself the

maiden Ruth, the arms of the young men drawing into the barns the grain. It is a moment of imaginative splendor and depth.[13]

The transformation that occurs between the beginning and the ending of the story is captured in the contrast between the book's images of famine and harvest. Emptiness and fullness are pervasive human experiences; on this level the book touches deep chords in us. We remember times when our own longing and darkness have issued in a harvest of comfort, peace, or new understanding. We recall seasons of thanksgiving, and unexpected joys, experiences of the goodness of God and the fullness of God's love. The story unveils for us the presence of grace in the midst of ordinary human activities, and of life coming out of death. This is what its symbols reveal. They invite us to find God in the seasons of our lives.

Attentiveness to the artistic qualities of a text also rewards our reading of an ancient and familiar narrative, the saga of Abraham's sacrifice of Isaac in Genesis 22:1–19.[14] The austere beauty of this story demands disciplined attention to its language and imagery. We wonder as we approach the text: What does Abraham feel? What is he thinking? The author does not give us a minute description of Abraham's emotional state in face of what seems a monstrous command. To understand his feelings we must read carefully in verse 6 how Abraham carries the fire and knife in his own hands and gives the wood to Isaac so that his son will not be exposed to any harm. Then, as Abraham and Isaac approach the place of sacrifice, the narrative tempo slows. Through this slower pace and the build-up of verbs, we sense the tensions within Abraham.

When they arrived at the place God had pointed out to him, Abraham built an altar there, and arranged the wood.

> Then he bound his son Isaac and put him on the altar on
> top of the wood. Abraham stretched out his hand and
> seized the knife to kill his son (9–10).

The language is at once more exact and more hesitant. The
arresting simplicity of these sentences is fraught with the
depth and complexity of Abraham's decision.

The characters of Abraham and Isaac and their relationship to God are also revealed through the skillful use of
dialogue. In the dialogue which opens the story we hear God's
call and command, and Abraham's readiness to respond. In the
description of Isaac there are also echoes of the larger story
surrounding this narrative. The history and destiny of many
are centered in this one child. Abraham had no heir and was
given a child after long years of waiting.

> It happened some time later that God put Abraham to the
> test. "Abraham, Abraham," he called. "Here I am," he
> replied. "Take your son," God said, "your only child
> Isaac, whom you love, and go to the land of Moriah.
> There you shall offer him as a burnt offering, on a moun-
> tain I will point out to you" (1–2).

Isaac is the child of promise, the future of Israel. Will God
abandon the promise? This opening dialogue generates a tension between the divine plan and its ostensible failure to be
fulfilled. The tension will be released only as the story's
conclusion makes clear that what God wants is faith and trust,
not human sacrifices. The story fuses literary art and theological vision, showing us by almost wordless restraint Abraham as
paradigm of obedience and the steadfastness of God's promise.

As we are drawn into this narrative we begin to experience it as a revelation for us. We see the story of Abraham and
Isaac as our story. Are we Isaac? Are we Abraham? Elie Wiesel
calls it a story of fear, faith, defiance and laughter. "Why," he

asks, "was the most tragic of our ancestors named Isaac, a name which evokes and signifies laughter? Here is why. As the first survivor, he had to teach us, the future survivors of Jewish history, that it is possible to suffer and despair an entire lifetime and still not give up the art of laughter."[15] Through the symbolic disclosure that occurs in this biblical narrative, we see that God can lead his people into darkness, but that he also changes suffering into blessing. We understand what it means to be called and guided by God, and we see that God's promises endure in spite of all apparent failures. What is more, these truths are not abstract convictions for us. Through the narrator's skill, such revelation becomes personal and comprehensible. It takes a powerful and enduring hold on our imagination.

We have been listening to the Books of Ruth and Genesis to see how an artistic reading of the texts of Scripture can open us to the power of their themes and images. Attentiveness to image and metaphor is even more crucial in reading the poetry of the Scriptures. The Song of Songs, for example, is a cluster of metaphors and images: wine, perfume, oil, sun, vineyards, flocks, earrings, necklaces, myrrh, henna flowers, turtledoves, pomegranates, honeycomb. Through these sensuous images we are invited to delight in the joy of human love. Themes of absence and presence, of losing and finding, are interwoven with these to point up the striving toward union between man and woman:

> On my bed, at night, I sought him
> whom my heart loves.
> I sought but did not find him.
> So I will rise and go through the City;
> in the streets and the squares
> I will seek him whom my heart loves.
> . . . I sought but did not find him.

> The watchmen came upon me
> on their rounds in the City:
> "Have you seen him whom my heart loves?"
>
> Scarcely had I passed them
> than I found him whom my heart loves.
> I held him fast, nor would I let him go
> till I had brought him
> into my mother's house,
> into the room of her who conceived me (3:1–4).

The meaning of the poem comes through its images and they are powerful communicators of emotion, of what it feels like to be lovers. These images convey a vision of the sexes as equal, of a situation where the woman as well as the man takes the initiative. The Song of Songs' images also invite comparison with the poetry of the first chapters of Genesis: the garden, the themes of paradise, man, woman, nature, and the tensions of union and separation. Paradise is lost in Genesis. In the Song of Songs, we see that paradise survives in the world through love, and is rediscovered through love.[16]

Images are associative and relational and operate on many levels of meaning. Their power can be seen, for example, in the poetry of the prophet Jeremiah. A key image in Jeremiah is that of water, in contrast to dryness. He complains to God:

> Why is my suffering continual,
>   my wound incurable,
>   refusing to be healed?
> Do you mean to be for me a deceptive stream
>   with inconstant waters? (15:18).

Jeremiah distinguishes between God as the "fountain of living water" and those broken cisterns which allow the water to seep away. In another contrast he speaks of the desert shrub and the tree planted "by the waterside." At the end of his drought poem in 14:1—17:13, Jeremiah refers to those who forsake God and turn away from him. Their names will be written in the dust because "they have abandoned the fountain of living water" (17:13). By means of these contrasting images Jeremiah calls us to a deep inner conversion. We are to realize that apart from God, all is drought and dust.

Jeremiah's images of water and drought show us that an image contains many layers of meaning. Because of this power of the imagination to connect and relate, to "free associate," reading the Bible in terms of its images and patterns often sets in motion a process of remembering. Just as the image of the garden in the Song of Songs calls up the garden of Genesis, so the image of the stranger in the Book of Ruth reminds us of a familiar theme in the Hebrew Scriptures:

> You must not molest the stranger and oppress him, for
> you lived as strangers in the land of Egypt (Ex 22:21).

Each use of the image of stranger is deepened by these wider associations. Likewise the image of water found in Jeremiah's poetry takes on new meaning through its many biblical echoes. Water is, for example, the dominating image in the poetry of Psalm 42. Here the image is used both as the water of life and the water of death: "My soul thirsts for God, the God of life" (42:2); "Deep is calling to deep as your cataracts roar; all your waves, your breakers have rolled over me" (42:7). The images ultimately initiate that process of analogy whereby we see similarities and contrasts with our own experience, and this is their main function. For this reason Hans-Georg Gadamer calls the Bible a classic. For Gadamer, a classic is "that which speaks in such a way that it is not a statement about what is past, a mere testimony to something that still needs to be interpreted, but says something to the present as if it were said specially to it."[17] Continued reading of the Bible lets God's revelation illumine the enigmas of our lives. Our reading always remains unfinished. We can return continually to the biblical texts as new sources of understanding and love.

This power of the text depends on our deepening insight into its meaning. We reach the deeper significance of symbolic texts only through their direct and primary significance. That is the way all symbols function. This fact underscores the importance of our second guide for reading Scripture.

2. *Call on Historical and Literary Criticism for Assistance*

In our attentive listening to a text, the tools of historical and literary criticism can be of great help. There may be terms and customs which are not familiar to us. In the Zacchaeus passage, for example, it is helpful to understand the role of Jewish tax collectors in the first century and their alignment with foreign oppression. It is useful to know how high a sycamore tree is and whether you can see through its branches. In reading the Book of Ruth it is likewise helpful to know the status of the Moabites as foreigners in Israel's eyes, and the laws which give the poor the right to some of the gleanings of a harvest. We do need historical background. Its purpose, however, is to assist us in understanding the text. It never becomes primary. Astute literary criticism likewise serves a useful function. It can unlock the themes and images of a book and help us recognize the deeper structures in the text. But none of this substitutes for the encounter with the text itself.

Knowledge and study guide our reading of the Bible in another way. They help us deal with two concerns we have about approaching Scripture directly. The first is a fear of fundamentalism. We may be afraid that reading the text of the Bible itself will result in taking it too literally. However, imagination prevents such a literal reading; it is precisely what fundamentalism lacks. Asking of a biblical book like Revelation questions about the exact date and time of Jesus' coming results in a flattening of the book's imagery and poetry. Imagination is opposed to such a leveling of the richness of reality. Attention to the literary qualities of a text, rather than resulting in too literal a reading, leads to the recognition that truth is not simple, but complex. Further, we realize that there is more than one kind of truth. In addition to the truth of history and factual truth, there is the truth of myth, story, poetry, and proverb. This kind of truth is opposed to fundamentalism's tendency toward indoctrination and judgment. Truth conveyed in such forms as symbol and narrative is an invitation to respond in freedom. We are asked to enter sympathetically into the scene or symbol, to identify ourselves, for example, with actors who often display frailty, uncertainty, and sinfulness. Only such imaginative participation permits us to break out of judgment categories.

In addition to a fear of taking texts too literally, we may be afraid that if we approach biblical passages directly we will miss the message of the text. We want to know what *the* message of a book is. What is *the* truth which a certain passage teaches? We fear subjectivism. However, a passage may not teach one simple and single truth. Our reading may suggest several possible meanings of a passage, each of which is supported by the text itself. Paul Ricoeur speaks of this as a "surplus of meaning." An exact and literal meaning evades us because the text is overflowing. This is an indication of the richness of the biblical message. But to say that a text or image allows for many meanings is not to say that we are allowed to read anything at all into it. A text may permit a plurality of meanings, but it has its own laws which forbid other readings. As Paul Ricoeur has said:

> If it is true that there is always more than one way of
> construing a text, it is not true that all interpretations are

equal. The text presents a limited field of possible constructions.[18]

A text does not mean anything we might like it to mean. Part of the validation of its meanings comes from the interaction of the threads of its tapestry, the characters, themes, images, and action. A text is also validated by its context within a community of faith. This brings us to our last guide for reading.

3. *Celebrate and Live the Text within a Community of Faith*

Reading a biblical text within a community provides a context for the sharing and comparing of interpretations. This is a support as well as a corrective for our individual efforts to read the Bible. A text often comes alive for us as we listen to another's insights into it. At other times, a community will challenge and clarify an interpretation we have given to a particular passage. Community is also the context for two intrinsic elements in understanding the word of God: celebration and action. In his 1979 presidential address to the Catholic Biblical Association, "Hermeneutics and the Teaching of Scripture," George T. Montague includes celebration and action as the final steps in interpreting and teaching Scripture. On the importance of celebration for understanding, he says:

> Most of the biblical texts, as most religious texts in general, were created in one way or another as scripts for celebration, and thus there is a surplus of meaning which the text, like the tip of the iceberg, only suggests, and which reliving in ritual alone can reveal.[19]

For many Christians of earlier ages it was preaching and ritual, cathedral windows and morality plays, not the study of the text, which completed their circle of understanding. The biblical passages are meant to be read, prayed, sung, dramatized. This is done best in a community of believers.

The final test of the Christian community's understanding of a biblical text is the living of its truth. As James and John insist in their New Testament letters, we must learn to do the truth in love. Action within a community of faith alone enables us to understand the final meaning of a passage. Sandra Schneiders concludes her interpretation of the foot washing scene in John 13:1–20 by stressing that one aspect of a valid interpretation of the scene is its significance for a contemporary disciple of Jesus. Jesus' washing of the disciples' feet enables us to understand Christian ministry "as a participation in Jesus' work of transforming the sinful structures of domination operative in human society according to the model of friendship expressing itself in joyful mutual service unto death."[20] We have not completely understood Scripture until it transforms us. We have not asked the right questions of the Scriptures until they question us.

When we read the Bible within a community of faith we also discover that these texts continually undergo reinterpretation. A study of the history of texts shows us how they have spoken to and been shaped by new situations. Phyllis Trible in her study of *God and the Rhetoric of Sexuality* follows what she calls "the pilgrimage of an ancient portrait of God," the text of Exodus 34:6–7:

> Yahweh, Yahweh, a God merciful and gracious, slow to anger, and abounding in loyalty and faithfulness, keeping loyalty for thousands, forgiving iniquity and transgression and sin, but who will by no means clear the guilty, visiting the iniquity of the ancestors upon the children and the children's children, to the third and fourth generation.[21]

The text holds in tension the punishment and the love of God. Trible shows how different formulations of it appeared in different settings of Israel's history. Moses is depicted as repeating the portrait of God in a prayer, omitting a few phrases (Num 14:8). Jeremiah quotes a condensed version of it as a prayer (Jer 32:18). With the prophet Joel, all the references to the anger of God disappear from the passage (Jl 2:13). The psalmists repeat and paraphrase the passage, fitting it in each case to a particular occasion and experience, whether it be thanksgiving, hymn, or individual lament (Ps 111:4; 112:4; 145:8). After the exile the passage becomes a message of comfort to a defeated people, having lost its allusions to the punishing God (Na 1:5).

Following the journey of this text within Israel's story shows us that interpretation invites us to participate in the movement of a biblical text. The word of God lives by dynamic analogy. A text has been interpreted in the community of faith over many generations, and one generation may discover something that another has missed. The text speaks to different hearers in different contexts and reveals a variety of methodologies: confession, additions, omissions, irony. The pilgrimage of such a text is a clue to the pilgrimage of the Bible in the world. The history of biblical passages shows us how the text comes to life for a community of faith, and gives us clues to the dynamic nature of the word of God which bridges historical gaps.

This is what is meant by *hearing* the word. John's Gospel speaks of such hearing as dwelling or remaining in God's word.

> To the Jews who believed in him Jesus said: "If you make my word your home you will indeed be my disciples, you will learn the truth and the truth will make you free" (8:31–32).

When we dwell in the word, making it our home, it becomes a living power in our lives. Since God's self-disclosure takes place in symbol, dwelling in the word is an act of the imagination. We do not try to put ourselves back into past history. We rely on what William Beardslee refers to as a story's capacity to bring "a remembered past into the present."[22] John also stresses that abiding in God's word is intimately connected with keeping the commandments in a spirit of love (15:10). We begin with attentive listening to the word itself, in the context of a community of ritual and action. We use all the guidance that literary and historical criticism can provide for hearing the word. Then the final test of our understanding of Scripture is our willingness to witness to it in life.

Notes

1. *Early Christian Rhetoric. The Language of the Gospel* (rev. ed.; Cambridge: Harvard U. Press, 1971), p. 118.

2. (2nd ed.; New Jersey: Prentice-Hall, 1966), p. 7.

3. "The Symbolic Structure of Revelation," *Theological Studies* 41/1 (March 1980), 55–56. I am indebted to Dulles' fine analysis of the sources of revelation.

4. "Symbols Are Actions, Not Objects," *Living Worship* 13/2 (February 1977), 1.

5. "Toward a Hermeneutic of the Idea of Revelation." In *Essays on Biblical Interpretation*, ed. Lewis S. Mudge (Philadelphia: Fortress Press, 1980), pp. 98–104.

6. *The Meaning of Revelation* (New York: Macmillan Co., 1941).

7. *Early Christian Rhetoric,* p. 127.

8. "Story and History in Biblical Theology," *Journal of Religion* 56/1 (January 1976), 1–17.

9. (Philadelphia: Fortress Press, 1970), pp. 1–13.

10. (New York: Vintage Books, 1973), pp. 6–7.

11. My discussion is based on the approach to this passage by Walter Vogels, "Structural Analysis and Pastoral Work," *Lumen Vitae* 33/4 (1978), 482–492.

12. See D.F. Rauber, "Literary Values in the Book of Ruth," *Journal of Biblical Literature* 89 (March 1970), 27–37.

13. "Literary Values in the Book of Ruth," 33.

14. For helpful suggestions on such reading see Robert Alter, *The Art of Biblical Narrative* (New York: Basic Books, Inc., 1981), and Gerhard Lohfink, *The Bible: Now I Get It!* (New York: Doubleday & Co., 1979), pp. 84–92.

15. *Messengers of God. Biblical Portraits & Legends,* trans. Marion Wiesel (New York: Random House, 1976), p. 86.

16. This comparison is developed by Francis Landy in "The Song of Songs and the Garden of Eden," *Journal of Biblical Literature* 98/4 (December 1979), 513–528.

17. *Truth and Method* (New York: Seabury Press, 1975), p. 257.

18. *Interpretation Theory: Discourse and the Surplus of Meaning* (Fort Worth: Texas Christian U. Press, 1976), p. 79.

19. *Catholic Biblical Quarterly* 41/1 (January 1979), 16.

20. "The Foot Washing (John 13:1–20): An Experiment in Hermeneutics," *Catholic Biblical Quarterly* 43/1 (January 1981), 91.

21. (Philadelphia: Fortress Press, 1978). Trible uses the RSV translation of this passage as quoted here.

22. *Literary Criticism of the New Testament,* p. 16.

III. Spirituality and the Arts

Works of art are the fruit of the imagination. Hence, the role of artists is central, not peripheral, to Christian existence. Yet many Christians, while acknowledging the close connection between religion and art in past centuries, still view art as merely a useful or pleasant adornment to faith. Artists build us beautiful churches and decorate them. They provide music and dance to enhance our worship. They give us portraits of Jesus. However, for many, the center of faith lies elsewhere, in creed and doctrine.

The relationship between faith and the arts is deeper and more pervasive than is generally acknowledged. All artists, not simply those who treat Christian themes, affect our Christian spirituality. In this section we will see why Christian faith cannot survive if it is isolated from the artists of its age.

As a framework for considering this relationship between spirituality and the arts, let us look at the reflections of a painter. We will use a passage from *My Name Is Asher Lev,* Chaim Potok's novel which traces the development of a Hasidic Jew as he becomes a talented contemporary painter. Toward the end of the novel, Asher describes how he has walked for hours on the streets of Brooklyn pondering the meaning of his gifts as an artist:

Sometime during the walking, I stopped in front of a mound of snow and with my finger drew in one continu-

ous line the contour of my face. Asher Lev in snow on a
Brooklyn parkway. Asher Lev, Hasid. Asher Lev, painter.
I looked at my right hand, the hand with which I painted.
There was power in that hand. Power to create and
destroy. Power to bring pleasure and pain. Power to
amuse and horrify. . . . Asher Lev paints good pictures and
hurts people he loves. Then be a great painter, Asher Lev;
that will be the only justification for all the pain you will
cause. But as a great painter I will cause pain again if I
must. Then become a greater painter. But I will cause pain
again. Then become a still greater painter. Master of the
Universe, will I live this way all the rest of my life? Yes,
came the whisper from the branches of the trees. Now
journey with me, my Asher. Paint the anguish of all the
world. Let people see the pain. But create your own molds
and your own play of forms for the pain. We must give a
balance to the universe.[1]

These reflections on a Brooklyn parkway suggest three
links between spirituality and the arts. "Let people see," the
Master of the Universe responds to Asher Lev, even as he
struggles with the consequences of opening people's eyes. The
arts reveal. Artists open the way to contemplation by showing
us hidden qualities of our inner and outer worlds.

"Create your own molds and your own play of forms,"
the Master continues. Artists in each age provide living forms
for our faith. They challenge us, in turn, to find new ways to
express our spiritual experiences. "We must give a balance to
the universe," the Master of the Universe concludes. The
world is searching for a lost harmony. The arts are key to a
kind of unity which holds differences together in a harmonious
pattern. This is the unity we call beauty. Artistic expression in
music, art, dance, drama, and literature is therefore central to
a recovery of human balance and wholeness. In turn, the
vision that comes from lives rooted in the Transcendent can

instill fresh hope and healing in the artistic imagination of our time. This concern for wholeness and harmony underlies our interest in these three bonds between spirituality and the arts.

Let People See

John's Gospel depicts Christian life as a new way of seeing. The second sign performed by Jesus in Jerusalem is the cure of the man born blind (9:1–41). Jesus opens the eyes of the blind and calls all people to accept the gift of sight. The concluding conversation between Jesus and the man shows that the most important part of the cure is not the man's having regained physical sight, but his coming to the spiritual insight of faith: "Jesus heard they had driven him away, and when he found him he said to him, 'Do you believe in the Son of Man?' 'Sir,' the man replied, 'tell me who he is so that I may believe in him.' Jesus said, 'You are looking at him; he is speaking to you.' The man said, 'Lord, I believe,' and worshipped him" (35–38). The blindness which refuses to see God at work is worse than congenital blindness. Believing is also seeing, since the believer has passed from the darkness of this world into light (Jn 1:4–5). To see with fresh eyes is to receive the graces found in the depths of ordinary life. St. Paul, in his own description of faith, reminds us that we see God reflected in the things that are made (Rom 1:20). The very commonness of daily life harbors the marvel and mystery of God's grace. Such is the message of the Incarnation.

Artists are essential to faith because without them we cannot truly see ourselves and our universe. They will not let us bypass the world on our way to God. Rather, they show us that revelation comes through the concrete particulars of this world. The novelist Robert Penn Warren calls this link between the life of art and of religion "humility": "Both (art and religion) depend on revelation, and both recognize that revelation comes only from a prayerful reverence for the truth, especially from an unscared reverence for the shockingness of inner truth."[2] Art confronts us with this truth in several ways, and it requires humility to take it in.

Artists are capable of revealing us to ourselves with relentless clarity. At times they force us to recognize truths we would rather keep hidden: our human anguish, our loneliness, our potential for planetary destruction. Along with the doubt and emptiness, however, they reveal the human capacity for freedom, honesty and courage. Each artist presents us with some particular self-understanding or some understanding of human existence for our consideration. The theologian Paul Tillich speaks of Picasso's "Guernica" as a great contemporary religious painting. It is a mural of human cruelty and wreckage. It is also a dream of justice. Tillich considers "Guernica" perhaps the most outstanding example of an artistic expression of, and protest against, the predicament of our time. It puts before us with tremendous power the question of our human world of guilt, anxiety and despair.[3]

The Swiss painter Paul Klee titled one of his works, "Destruction and Hope." He painted it in 1916, when he was surrounded by the decay and collapse of the war years, and it portrays life at the transition point between yesterday and tomorrow, destruction and hope. Saul Bellow's novel *Henderson the Rain King* portrays an American millionaire so dedicated to solitary self-realization that he flees any attachments or loyalties. Yet even in the remote African wilderness he cannot escape the need for some encounter with reality. Such varied visions of the human are the continual concern of Christian spirituality, because they show us how the Christian call to decision and action can be lived out in the actual circumstances of our era. Spirituality is not one compartment or sphere of life. It is, rather, a style of life, the process of life itself lived with the vision of faith. On the occasion of his

Nobel award in 1957, Albert Camus summed up this power of artistic revelation by referring to his own art as an attempt to stir people by providing them images of our joys and woes. Unless Christians listen to the artists of their time, they will be unable to assess either the sickness or the health of the human situation.

The artist does not reveal the world to us in propositions and measurements. The artist shows us the rich and irreducible particulars of existence. In this way we are held fast to the earth as we search for God. The painter Vincent Van Gogh describes the importance of such attention to individual things. In a letter to his brother Theo, Vincent remarks that he finds himself pondering again and again the Gospel saying that there are those who have ears but do not hear, have eyes but do not see, and have a heart but do not feel, because their heart is hardened and they have closed their ears and eyes. In this same letter Vincent describes how he has been working on a painting of a weed burner, trying to capture the gathering twilight, the immensity of the plain, the fire with its bit of smoke as the only light. He says that he has gone again and again to look at it in the evening.

Van Gogh marvels that things are so full of character and so varied that they call out for someone to paint them. In a later letter to Theo he describes what he has seen on his trip to Zweeloo:

> The broad-fronted houses here stand between oak trees of a splendid bronze. In the moss are tones of gold bronze; in the ground, tones of reddish, or bluish or yellowish dark lilac gray; in the green of the cornfields, tones of inexpressible purity; on the wet trunks, tones of black, contrasting with the golden rain of whirling, clustering autumn leaves—hanging in loose tufts, as if they had been blown there, and with the sky glimmering through them—from the poplars, the birches, the lime and apple trees.[4]

The artist recovers the splendor of the world for us, enabling us to see what might remain inchoate and inarticulate because of our less sensitive sight or our preoccupation with other things. Such an ability to see is the basis for a spirituality which rejoices with the Hebrew psalmist in praise of the wonder and variety of creation. It is also the basis for the receptive and attentive style of living which prepares us to receive the gifts of God as they come to us through the world.

The artist's power can present the individual, irreducible aspects of reality in such a way that they open us to the depth in reality.[5] Contemplation of the visible puts us in touch with the invisible, the divine Depth in all created things. This is the vision of the poet Gerard Manley Hopkins, who writes that "the world is charged with the grandeur of God. It will flame out, like shining from shook foil."[6] Hopkins passionately sought the living God. He found him in the miraculous singularity and uniqueness of all things. A lay brother at Stonyhurst, the seminary to which Hopkins went after taking his vows as a Jesuit, tells of seeing Hopkins after a shower run and crouch down to study the glint of some quartz in the path as the sun came out and shone upon it.[7] The particularity of each thing in creation fascinated Hopkins. In his poem *Pied Beauty* he glories in dappled things—skies, brindled cows, rose-moles, trout, fire-coals, chestnut-falls, finches' wings, landscapes plotted. God's beauty shines forth through all of these. Finally, the Incarnation transforms Hopkins' ultimate vision of things. All disclose the presence of Christ in their "isness" and "suchness":

> For Christ plays in ten thousand places,
> Lovely in limbs, and lovely in eyes not his
> To the Father through the features of men's faces.[8]

Hopkins saw all of life as sacramental.

This mystery of the universal in the particular, of the Whole found in individual things, finds expression in Japanese art in the way an artist may spend time studying a single blade of grass. The blade of grass leads the artist to draw all plants, the seasons, and then the human figure. An entire lifetime is not enough to contemplate and celebrate such wonders. The "eye is the lens of the heart, open to the world," says the Zen artist Frederick Franck. "For the artist-within (who must exist in everyone, for if man is created in God's image, it can only mean that he is created creative) there is no split between his seeing, art, and 'religion' in the sense of realizing his place in the fabric of all that is."9

The artist, then, introduces us to the depth dimensions of human experience. Unless these dimensions are clad in flesh and blood, the eye is unable to see them. The artist enables us to see and hear by finding new forms for familiar content. Through the creation of poems, legends, mosaics, carvings, paintings, songs, and sculptures, the artist, in a sense, makes the world stand still long enough for us to glimpse its mystery.

Create Your Own Molds and Your Own Play of Forms

Artists are makers of form. They share in their own way in incarnation, the embodiment of spirit in matter. Christian spirituality needs the arts because such symbolic expression is vital to personal growth. Alfred North Whitehead calls expression "the one fundamental sacrament. It is the outward and visible sign of an inward and spiritual grace."10 Every deep emotion carries an urge to be projected; even the deep feelings of a solitary individual include an impulse to be shared. Spirit must be embodied in matter: words, stone, music, paint, poetry. By giving form to spiritual content, artists enrich Christian life in several ways: (1) they make our experiences accessible to us; (2) they show us the goodness as well as the limits of the material universe; (3) they revitalize lifeless symbols and images; (4) they challenge us to create new forms of expression for our own spiritual experiences. Let us examine more closely each of these ways in which artists give form to our faith.

We cannot apprehend our experiences of joy and pain, fear and courage, belief and doubt, until they find expression. We can appropriate only the life or vision which is adequately embodied in sensuous materials. As Theseus says in Shakespeare's *A Midsummer-Night's Dream:*

> And, as imagination bodies forth
> The forms of things unknown, the poet's pen
> Turns them to shapes, and gives to airy nothing
> A local habitation and a name (V, 1).

Without a definite form, experience remains vague. It recedes from awareness and is difficult to capture again. Artists attempt to give form to the flux and confusion of experience, making it accessible to us. We have all known the flash of recognition that comes from finding our perceptions of human love, suffering, or community fleshed out for us in a novel, a poem, or the movements of a symphony.

The most common symbols of the spiritual life are words. They embody our religious intentions, feelings, and emotions; they give shape and limit to our thoughts. We pray with words; we use words to describe our religious experiences. But our most profound experiences break the bonds of words alone. So artists give form to the aspirations of the human spirit in a variety of other ways. As a means of expressing his thanks to God for his recovery from illness Beethoven composes the String Quartet in A Minor. The Gothic cathedral is an expression of medieval religious sentiment in a structure of stone. The opening up of the cathedral's interior space into communion with infinite reaches expresses a yearning for union with

God, and its interstices are filled with stained glass windows whose colors are not self-contained and hold no splendor unless a distant light shines through them.[11]

Another artistic form which is reclaiming its position of importance in spirituality, especially in prayer and worship, is the dance. Dance has been a part of all dimensions of the process of life: harvesting, worship, birth, death, love, marriage, battle, and victory. When the ark of God is finally returned to Jerusalem, David and all the house of Israel dance before God "with all their might, singing to the accompaniment of lyres, harps, tambourines, castanets and cymbals" (2 Sam 6:5–6). The movement of dance is able to give material shape to the total range of human emotions and feelings. It calls for participation as a prelude to understanding, but to share in the dance one need only bring one's self; no other materials are necessary. Further, as the phenomenologist of religion Gerardus Van Der Leeuw reminds us,

> the dance is not something in which we can participate or not, as we like. Whoever does not dance runs, races, waddles, limps—that is, he dances badly. We must learn once more to dance, so that once again a general consciousness of life can be created, and finally perhaps even a style of life.[12]

When religion and the arts stood in greater unity with one another, dance was worship, just as song was prayer. Dance—beautiful, frenzied, agonized, or calm—gives expression in a total way to the rhythm of the self before God, others, and the mysteries of life.

By embodying spirit in forms that captivate our attention, artists nourish our sense of the sacramentality of life. They also contribute to this sacramental vision by showing us the power and the limits of the material universe. They remind us of the holiness of the earth, yet root us in reality as it is.

An artist works with the materials of the world and reveals the qualities inherent in commonplace things. Through Michelangelo's figures we come to appreciate the simplest human gesture. The sculptor Henry Moore uses the graining and fine surfaces of wood, the strength of bronze, and the openness of space as the stuff of sculpture. Calder's sculpture plays with stress, balance, motion, and time-rhythms. Noguchi exploits the translucence and glow of marble. Other artists work with the color, texture, and shape of things. The materials are as varied as the forms. Perhaps no artistic exploration of an element of the material universe is as striking as Rembrandt's moving pictorial expression of light. In his discussion of art and visual perception Rudolf Arnheim describes Rembrandt's use of the symbolism of light:

> In Rembrandt's paintings, the objects receive light passively as the impact of an outer force, but at the same time they become light sources themselves, actively radiating energy. Having become enlightened, they hand on the message. . . . Rembrandt enables a book or a face to send out light without violating the requirements of a realistic style of painting. By this pictorial device he copes with the central mystery of the Gospel story, the light that has become matter.[13]

Working closely with the natural order, artists affirm for us its goodness and potential.

Artistic form also teaches us respect for limits. Artistic creativity exists under certain restrictions which set it free. The philosopher Alfred North Whitehead has called creativity the principle of novelty, but he points out that limitation is the key to its existence. The artist must produce the new within the restrictions imposed by material symbols and conditions. Anne Sexton says it of words, but it it applies as well to all other materials of creation.

Yet often they fail me.
I have so much I want to say,
so many stories, images, proverbs, etc.
But the words aren't good enough,
the wrong ones kiss me.
Sometimes I fly like an eagle
but with the wings of a wren.[14]

The struggle to embody spirit in matter reveals both the power of the material universe and the transcendence of spirit.

The respect for discipline and limits found in artistic creation also reminds us of an important dimension of all spiritual expression. Just as form frees artistic creativity, so do certain limitations open us to the Spirit. This is true on the personal level, as attested by the disciplines associated with the great contemplative traditions. Control of the mind, body, or breathing can open us to deeper levels of religious experience. The principle applies as well to our community prayer. Artists illustrate for us the important role that rhythm and form play in our liturgy. A service that is carelessly put together hinders our common prayer. Just as setting certain boundaries allows creative depths to come to expression, so giving definite structure to our communal worship frees the spirit.

By creating their own molds and play of forms artists increase our understanding of incarnation and sacrament in these first two ways: they capture the deepest experiences of the human spirit, and they sharpen our awareness of the qualities of our material world. As we shall see, they also find living forms for our faith and challenge us to do the same. In this way art is not only expressive of our thoughts and feelings; it has power to evoke them. Let us examine this further.

One function of religious symbols and images is to link us with the tradition. The cross and the madonna with child, the kingdom and the covenant, unite us with our religious past and commit us to a common heritage. But that is not their only purpose. They also evoke the sacred. Such symbols and images have power to open new horizons, calling forth in our minds and hearts the very presence of Mystery. However, as symbols such as the cross become more and more familiar to us, they lose this evocative power. We have seen certain depictions of the crucifixion so often that they have lost their power to shock our sensibilities. Or we have heard the Genesis account of creation so many times that it no longer conveys the mystery of the event. Symbols and images die. As Christians we find ourselves the possessors of a heap of broken images and symbols that lack power to give life to our faith. This is often the result of Christianity's isolation from the creative artists of its age.

Artists bring new life to our traditional symbols. They do this by removing their familiar faces and placing them in new contexts. Since dead forms frequently result from the pressures of familiarity, artists must first strip away the familiar features of an object before we can see it anew. The gifted American fiction writer Flannery O'Connor, when asked about the bizarre characters inhabiting many of her stories, replied:

> When you can assume that your audience holds the same beliefs you do, you can relax a little and use more normal ways of talking to it; when you have to assume that it does not, then you have to make your vision apparent by shock—to the hard of hearing you shout, and for the almost blind you draw large and startling figures.[15]

Flannery O'Connor wanted her fiction to stir the modern imagination to fresh life. She challenges a secular world which has lost a sense of the sacred to new awareness of the demands of the moral life.

This distancing from the familiar gives much contemporary art a prophetic character. A contemporary sculpture or painting will not always comfort; it may repel, upset, or make demands. "I can't help it," wrote the artist André Marchand, "if Christ for me is someone from Dachau, some twentieth-century man who has been humiliated, insulted, victimized, tracked to death or burned alive...."[16] Such a Christ, however, may unsettle the security we have found in our traditional images, many of them perhaps shaped largely by childhood associations. So also may the fiberglass figure of *Resurrection* by the American Jack Zajac. In contrast to traditional representations of the resurrection which show a totally glorified body cleansed of all traces of pain and death, Zajac's figure is informed by limpness and a tremendous sense of dead weight. The Christ figure is somewhat larger than life size, with a stiffness of arms and legs which attests death and hanging on the cross. Through his *Resurrection* Zajac wishes to imply that the risen Christ raises with him all the agony of the passion and death.[17] By this less common portrayal of the risen Christ Zajac compels us to reflect again on the theological truth of the resurrection of the body. A typical objection to such unconventional depictions of Christ was voiced to the French painter André Girard several years ago. A woman visitor to a chapel he had decorated told him, "M. Girard, I do not like your crucifixion; it is so unpleasant." "Madame," said the artist, "it was an unpleasant occasion."[18]

Another way that artists restore the power of our traditional symbols is by placing them in new settings. New meanings emerge from such recontextualizing. The story of the "Creation of Man" which is the subject of Michelangelo's ceiling of the Sistine Chapel in Rome is familiar to every reader of the Book of Genesis. But Michelangelo's rendering does not depict the Creator breathing a living soul into a body of clay. Rather, God reaches out toward the arm of Adam, transmitting from the Maker to the creature an animating spark which seems to leap from fingertip to fingertip. The forces of life-giving energy conveyed visibly through the energy-charged arm of God come alive in one who participates in this artistic portrayal of the Genesis story. The story of Cain and Abel is revitalized in the contemporary context provided by John Steinbeck in *East of Eden*. Here the reader enters anew into the mystery of the gift of free will and the human legacy of sin and grace. Poets also fill our minds with images by transmuting Christian symbols in their poetry. In T.S. Eliot's "East Coker," Adam becomes "the ruined millionaire":

> The whole earth is our hospital
> Endowed by the ruined millionaire. . . .[19]

The point is that our religious vision must be translated into the unique voice of a particular epoch if it is to support a living faith. For this translation we depend on the artists of our age.

Openness to the arts is itself an act of the imagination, a way in which our imaginations are educated. However, artists also challenge us as individuals and communities to create our own molds and play of forms, to be, as Nietzsche says, "the poets of our lives."[20] The art in this case is that of finding the form or style of spirituality which best expresses our faith. Applied to prayer, for example, this means the freedom to be ourselves before God, letting go of older forms of prayer which may have lost their meaning for us. The great men and women in the history of Christian spirituality illustrate vividly this ability to create forms of spirituality appropriate to their age: Francis of Assisi, Teresa of Avila, Ignatius Loyola, Catherine of Siena, Pierre Teilhard de Chardin, Simone Weil. So do the musicians and artists who have enriched Christian worship throughout history. Such search for living forms applies to all aspects of our life as a Christian community, including the architecture of our churches. As Clark B. Fitz-

Gerald says in "A Sculptor Discusses Contemporary Religious Work":

> If the elements of a church, its visual symbols, do not speak to us today, they are of little value. To build a church today with anything but a contemporary attitude can only result in the work being stillborn. I'm fully aware of the pain caused by a new idea; every creative person has struggled with it. Yet if our churches are to have real meaning today they must go through this same struggle.[21]

In dialogue with artists the Church must develop its own style and shape if it is effectively to preach in our era the message that the "Word was made flesh; he lived among us" (Jn 1:14).

We have reflected on two major ways in which artists are essential to Christian spirituality. First, they enable us to see, revealing our world to us in its individuality and depth. Then, as makers of form, they contribute to the development of a living faith, giving expression to our experience and finding forms which evoke faith anew. In all these ways artists are indispensable servants of an incarnational and sacramental spirituality. They support our faith in yet a third way. They offer us the order of beauty as key to the unity and harmony we seek.

We Must Give a Balance to the Universe

The influence of the arts is not limited to the power of individual artistic productions. The arts must shape the kind of community we become. The Russian-born painter Ben Shahn describes this power of artists to form our minds and sensibilities.

> I have always believed that the character of a society is largely shaped and unified by its great creative works, that

a society is molded upon its epics, and that it imagines in terms of its created things—its cathedrals, its works of art, its musical treasures. . . . [22]

One area where the arts can help us imagine new solutions is in our search for unity: How can individuals and communities achieve some kind of harmony?

The problem of the relationship between the individual and the community is an ancient and perplexing one. It takes many forms. St. Paul struggled with it in the early Christian community in Corinth and enunciated the principle that individual gifts are for the purpose of building up the community in love (1 Cor 12–13). Couples living out the marriage covenant also search for a kind of union which will at the same time deepen and harmonize the individuality of each partner. How can differences enhance rather than threaten the marriage bond? On a national and worldwide level we face the challenge of uniting diverse races and religious groups without destroying their uniqueness.

The arts cannot solve all dimensions of so vast and complex a problem. However, they can make a significant contribution toward its solution. Artists offer us beauty as a design for life. Alfred North Whitehead speaks of the order of beauty as a way of balancing the importance of both individuals and communities. Beauty is a harmony of contrasts. Each element in a pattern has its individual beauty; all contribute as well to the beauty of the whole. As an illustration of this, Whitehead refers to the Cathedral of Chartres. The sculptured figures on the Cathedral's porch retain their individuality while adding to the total beauty.[23] In a similar way, a symphony can achieve unity from the strong dynamic contrasts between notes, themes, or melodies. An artist is able to transform incompatible elements into compatible contrasts. In an artistic creation different sounds, shapes and colors mutually modify and mingle with one another. The artist's concern is with the individual and the specific, but also with the way in which two or more varied individuals can exist together.

That is the way to community. In a community of faith, beauty results when unique and strong individuals mutually enhance one another. The poet and paleontologist Teilhard de Chardin presents a similar vision for the universe in his Omega Point. Teilhard believed that true unity differentiates, that we become more deeply ourselves as we achieve union. Such unity demands that we come together not simply mind to mind or body to body, but heart to heart:

> Only union *through* love and *in* love ... because it brings individuals together, not superficially and tangentially but center to center, can physically possess the property of not merely differentiating but also personalizing the elements which comprise it.[24]

We need to transform our political, economic, social, and religious structures to the end of such beauty. Such transformation requires the enlarging of our sensibilities so that we come to view unity as a rainbow in the colors of all people. Rather than seeing those different from us as a threat, we need to discover that such differences can enrich community. "Everything can change if we pronounce the word love without shame," declared the nineteenth century Russian painter Marc Chagall. "The true spirit of art resides in love."[25] Artists provide us with a vision of the harmony of contrasts as the path to unity.

We have explored three links between spirituality and the arts: the capacity of the arts for revelation, for giving expression to our life of faith, and for providing us with patterns for unity. These are convincing reasons to close the gap which still exists between Christianity and the contemporary arts. In pondering the role of the artist in Christian spirituality we have seen that the challenge addressed to Asher Lev, in the passage from Chaim Potok's novel with which we began, is addressed to the artists of every age: "Let people see.... Create your own molds and your own play of forms.... We must give a balance to the universe." Art is not simply an adornment to a life of faith centered in creed and doctrine. We need painters, sculptors, dancers and musicians as much as theologians and philosophers. The arts belong at the heart of Christian life.

Notes

1. (New York: Alfred A. Knopf, 1972), pp. 367–368.

2. Foreword to *Christian Faith and the Contemporary Arts,* ed. Finley Eversole (New York: Abingdon Press, 1962), p. 8.

3. Paul Tillich, *Theology of Culture,* ed. Robert C. Kimball. (New York: Oxford U. Press, 1959), pp. 68–69.

4. Letters 335 and 340. In *The Complete Letters of Vincent Van Gogh,* II (Greenwich, Connecticut: New York Graphic Society, 1959), pp. 184, 209.

5. See Nathan A. Scott, Jr., "Poetry and Prayer," *Thought* 41 (Spring 1966), 61–80.

6. *Gerard Manley Hopkins. Poems and Prose,* ed. W. H. Gardner (Baltimore: Penguin Books, 1953), p. 27.

7. *The Journals and Papers of Gerard Manley Hopkins,* eds. Humphrey House and Graham Storey (London: Oxford U. Press, 1959), p. 408.

8. "Inversnaid." In *Gerard Manley Hopkins. Poems and Prose,* p. 51.

9. *The Zen of Seeing. Seeing/Drawing as Meditation* (New York: Vintage Books, 1973), p. 8.

10. Alfred North Whitehead, *Religion in the Making* (New York: The World Publishing Co., 1960), p. 127.

11. See C.R. Morey, *Christian Art* (New York: W.W. Norton & Co., 1935), pp. 16–49.

12. *Sacred and Profane Beauty. The Holy in Art,* trans. David E. Green (New York: Holt, Rinehart & Winston, 1963), p. 74.

13. *Art and Visual Perception. A Psychology of the Creative Eye* (Berkeley: U. of California Press, 1974), p. 325.

14. "Words." In *The Awful Rowing Toward God* (Boston: Houghton Mifflin Co., 1975), p. 71.

15. "The Fiction Writer and His Country." In *The Living Novel: A Symposium,* ed. Granville Hicks (New York: Collier Books, 1962), p. 163.

16. Quoted in Pie-Raymond Régamey, *Religious Art in the Twentieth Century* (New York: Herder & Herder, 1963), pp. 173–174.

17. Frank and Dorothy Getlein, *Christianity in Modern Art* (Milwaukee: The Bruce Publishing Co., 1961), pp. 162–163.

18. Recounted in *Christianity in Modern Art,* p. 162.

19. "East Coker." In *The Complete Poems and Plays. 1909–1950* (New York: Harcourt, Brace & World, 1952), p. 128.

20. *Joyful Wisdom,* trans. Thomas Common (New York: Frederick Ungar Publishing Co., 1960), p. 233.

21. *Christian Faith and the Contemporary Arts,* p. 201.

22. *The Shape of Content* (New York: Vintage Books, 1957), p. 45.

23. *Adventures of Ideas* (New York: The Free Press, 1967), p. 264.

24. *The Future of Man,* trans. Norman Denny (New York: Harper & Row, 1964), pp. 244–245.

25. Marie-Thérèse Souverbie, *Chagall,* trans. Wade Stevenson (New York: Leon Amiel Publisher, 1975), p. 28.

IV. Prayer and the Imagination

Every Christian's life of prayer is sustained in some way by the life of the imagination. Images may provide the very method of prayer and give sustenance to it. St. Ignatius Loyola introduces such a use of images in *The Spiritual Exercises* where he pays special attention to the place of imagination, memory, and emotions in prayer. Images supply a Christian context even for the experience of imageless prayer. Prayer is sometimes a speechless, wordless union occurring at a level deeper than the images and concepts of the surface mind. But an image may often trigger such an experience of prayer. As the sixteenth century mystic Teresa of Avila stresses, life's journey of prayer is long, and moments of imagelessness need to be understood and sustained in terms of the sacraments and other Christian symbols. Liturgy, Scripture, music, and art are essential to the total spiritual life of any Christian.

Images and metaphors furnish a means of expressing the experience of the inner life; they are also a way of introducing others to the practice of prayer. The sixteenth century Spanish mystic St. John of the Cross conveys his spiritual experiences in moving poems which speak of a dark night and a living flame of love. The title of one of the best known mystical classics, *The Cloud of Unknowing,* is itself a metaphor meant to convey the heart of the prayer experience it describes. The

Christian tradition's many expressions for prayer are all metaphors which help us grasp its meaning: silent communion of heart with heart, lifting of the mind to God, conversation, dialogue, friendship, attention, listening. All this illustrates that balance and richness in any path of Christian prayer depend on recognition and understanding of the role of the imagination. If we want to enliven and deepen our prayer life, we must look at the place the imagination holds in it.

The many ways of using our imaginations in prayer have in common certain characteristics: (1) Praying with the imagination teaches us to participate in the particular and the ordinary as a way to God. (2) Imaginative contemplation receives the word of God indirectly and in paradox. (3) Images center our awareness of God's presence within ourselves and in all of creation. Reflection on these three characteristics will show how the use of the imagination keeps prayer tied to life in this world. Such prayer flows from the meaning of creation and Incarnation.

The House of God

The New Testament exegete John Dominic Crossan calls a parable of Jesus "the house of God."[1] To experience the power of God, we must live in the details of the parable and dwell in its silences, spaces and challenges. The Word became flesh and pitched his tent here among us. God has come to dwell among all people. Prayer that springs from belief in the Incarnation does not take us out of ordinary reality, but more deeply into it. It reveals how ordinary human life and events move beyond themselves to the hidden mystery of God. The world of the parable is neither secular nor religious, but both at once.

Prayer which takes seriously both dimensions, the secular and the religious, our world and God's presence, calls for imaginative participation. As the poet William Blake believed, imagination is capable of a kind of double vision. It is able to perceive something simultaneously in at least two ways. When Blake gazed at the sun he saw not only something round, an object like a guinea; he also saw a large heavenly choir singing God's praises. Imagination spans the gap between matter and spirit, linking them together. Imaginative participation is a way to pray the parables, the psalms, passages from the Gospels, and events from our own past and future. Exploration of each will show why they call for such participation.

Current biblical study emphasizes two aspects of the Gospel parables which have important implications for Christian prayer.[2] First, the parable is central to Jesus' teaching. This parable form is itself more than accidentally related to Jesus' message. Jesus not only describes his relationship with God and assures us as his disciples that we also are invited into such a relationship. He gives us parables as a process through which we not only hear about that experience of God, but actually share in it. As a linguistic form the parable calls for participants who enter into and experience the word of God, not mere observers who analyze a situation from a safe distance.

The second point biblical scholars make about the parables is that they are extended metaphors. This means that they are stories of ordinary people and events which provide the context for the extraordinary, the Transcendent. A new and powerful word from the depths breaks forth in the intervals, surprises, and unusual turns of the parables. In the parables there are plantings and harvests, budding fig trees, fathers and sons, women baking bread, seeds growing into trees. In and through all of this we discover the presence of God coming as gift and miracle, the challenge of God reversing values and tidy schemes, the hiddenness and mystery of God's coming, bringing with it joy. As Gerhard Ebeling has said, "The art of the parable . . . is none other than that of bringing the hearer face to face with what it is to be human and thereby to make clear what it means for God to draw near."[3]

How can these insights make a difference in the way we pray the parables? Recognizing that a parable is a poetic metaphor, we do not try to solve and explain it. Rather, we let the parable interpret and change us. Following are four exercises which can take us into the heart of the parable to contemplate it from within:

Become the person in the parable of the Good Samaritan (Lk 10:29–37) who has been stripped and beaten by robbers and left to die at the side of the road. Experience grace and compassion coming to you from your enemy, a Samaritan. Feel the details of compassionate love as this stranger bandages your wounds, pours oil and wine on them, lifts you to a mount, carries you into an inn.

Imagine you are the lost sheep (Lk 15:4–7) cut off from the rest of the herd. You are confused and so paralyzed by fear that you cannot walk. Alone and with no means of saving yourself, your only hope is a shepherd who will care enough to search for you and carry you home. Know the joy of being rescued from the barren slopes, the storms, and wolves, and the relief of being restored to your group.

Identify with the one talent person in the parable of the talents (Mt 25:14–30). Watch yourself dig a hole in the ground to bury your talent safely. Feel your anxiety about losing your talent, your fear of risking it in any unknown and uncertain venture. Know the shock of discovering that your failure to trust and risk means you have lost your one talent.

Choose any of the parables and live in its details. Fall with the seed into the dark earth and grow slowly to the light again (Jn 12:24). Identify with one of the guest lists in the parable of the wedding feast (Mt 22:1–10). Search a field and experience the joy of finding an unexpected treasure (Mt 13:44–45). Feel gratitude at being forgiven freely and fully in spite of thoughtless living (Lk 15:11–32).

Identifying with new characters and parts of a parable helps to keep alive some of the freshness of its message.

We do not always approach parables in this way. We often analyze a parable to discover its meaning or point and then attempt to apply that meaning to our own life. The parable itself is on trial, not we, the hearers: Does it make sense? Are all its details complete and in place? In contrast, imaginative contemplation reminds us that a parable "does not *have* a message, it *is* a message."[4] Instead of our working on it, it works on us, enabling us to hear the good news in our own lives and to discover God at the center of life.

Imaginative participation also helps us to pray the psalms. The Hebrew psalms are poetry, filled with images. Trouble and distress find expression in Psalm 102:7–8.

I live in a desert like the pelican,
in a ruin like the screech owl.
I stay awake, lamenting
like a lone bird on the roof.

Longing for God is like parched land longing for water (Ps 63:2), a thirsty deer (Ps 42:1), like eating ashes or drinking tears (Ps 102:10). God's coming brings a new song to our hearts (Ps 40:3). As poetry, the psalms call for continual contemplation. We are to live into them in our prayer.

A distinctive feature of Hebrew poetry produces this contemplative awareness in us. In 1753 the Anglican bishop

Robert Lowth discovered the importance of parallelism as the key to Hebrew poetry. The single lines of the psalms are grouped in twos or threes according to parallelism of thought. This parallelism may be of several kinds. The second line may repeat the idea of the first.

> Come back, Yahweh, rescue my soul,
> save me, if you love me (Ps 6:5).

Or there may be a contrast between two statements.

> If you never overlooked our sins, Yahweh,
> Lord, could anyone survive?
> But you do forgive us: and for that we revere you
>   (Ps 130:3–4).

This contrast may make the same point in alternate ways.

> You turn your face away, they suffer.
> You stop their breath, they die and revert to dust.
> You give breath, fresh life begins, you keep renewing the
>   world (Ps 104:29–30).

Other psalms repeat a single theme over and over again in different words, using new illustrations. Themes such as a cry for help in danger (Ps 25) or the fate awaiting the good and the evil (Ps 37) appear throughout the psalms in new shapes and arrangements.

The parallelism of the psalms is a key to praying them. Just as the rhythm of music invites us to join in a dance, the rhythm of the psalms invites us to step into the text with our whole self. Parallelism creates a repetitive pattern, a kind of doubling back, which slows the movement of prayer and deepens contemplative experience. This poetic motion of the psalms is circular, in contrast to the sequential order of rational thought. When we are moving quickly from one idea to another, it is difficult to let any one thought sink in and deepen within us. By quietly reiterating a theme or image, a psalm calms our restless hearts and gently leads us into a prayerful attitude. Because it allows time for the psalmist's words to connect with our own experiences and feelings, this repetitive pattern calls for a response not only of the mind, but of the feelings and body as well.

Repetition in prayer is also a way of holding God in remembrance. The images of such prayer lodge deep within us and surface at other periods of our life, as with a woman who found herself praying the line, "The Lord is my shepherd, I shall not want," over and over again during a difficult hospital stay. The twentieth century mystic Simone Weil found that such repetition opened her to the gifts of God's presence in mystical prayer. These experiences came to her as she repeated the Our Father while working in a grape harvest in Ardèche, France.

Both parable and psalm can be the house of God, revealing the mystery and depth in ordinary concrete experience. One of the masters in guiding Christians to contemplate such individual events as a way of finding God in all things is St. Ignatius Loyola. In *The Spiritual Exercises* Ignatius focuses on the power found in limited images. Each aspect of the Gospel story is the object of contemplation: Jesus' baptism, the temptation, the call of the apostles, the miracle at Cana, the stilling of the storm at sea. Because of the unifying power of the imagination, we often move naturally from the Gospel scene to our own life during such contemplation: from a consideration of Jesus' temptation to our own temptations, from Christ's calming of the waves to our longing that he calm our storms. The imagination unifies past, present, and future in such a way that, although entry into a Gospel scene may appear to be a movement to the past, it is paradoxically a way of remaining in the present. This is similar to the Zen Buddhist attitude of attentiveness to ordinary objects and things in the here and now: a blade of grass, a flower in a vase. Such attentiveness leads to a total presence to reality.

Ignatius suggests that we hear, see, smell, taste, and touch in imagination what is taking place in a particular Christian mystery. When contemplating the birth of Jesus, we are "to see with the eyes of the imagination the road from Nazareth to Bethlehem; considering its length, breadth, and whether the way be level or through valleys and over hills."[5] Since emotional conversion is essential to internalizing the message of the Gospel, the prayer which flows from these contemplations expresses the amazement, confusion, sorrow, joy, peace, and love we feel. Ignatius considered the imagination and memory to be unruly powers, in need of control by the will. It is not necessary to agree with this view of the human person to use his method of praying the Gospel scenes by entering into them as participants.

Following Ignatius' lead, we can use our imaginations to bring the Gospel accounts to life. The following is such a contemplation of Mark 8:27–30, the confession of Peter at Caesarea Philippi.

Begin by sitting in a relaxed and comfortable position. Quiet yourself and breathe in and out deeply several times.

Read Mark 8:27–30.

Now imagine that you are with Jesus and several of his disciples in the village of Bethsaida where earlier Jesus cured a blind man. You are on the edge of the Sea of Galilee.

Notice the other disciples standing around waiting to begin the next journey. What do they look like? What are they saying?

Join them as they begin to walk north with Jesus to the villages around Caesarea Philippi. See the light of the early afternoon on the waters of the Sea of Galilee and the surrounding hills. Feel the sun on your back and the dust on your feet as you follow along the road with Jesus and the other disciples. What are you thinking as you move along?

After some time, Jesus begins to speak. You turn toward him and hear him say to you and the other disciples, "Who do people say I am?" What do you answer?

Hear the voice of one disciple as he replies, "John the Baptist." Then listen to the silence that follows. Hear another answer softly, "Others, Elijah." And listen as another says, "One of the prophets." What expression do you see on Jesus' face as he hears these answers?

Pause to hear the quiet sounds along the roadside. See the wheat shimmer in the warm sun. Then hear Jesus as he begins to speak. He turns to you and says, "But you, who do you say that I am?" How are you feeling as the question is put to you? What do you answer?

Finally, listen as Peter answers the question: "You are the Christ."

Take time to pray any prayers that have arisen in you as you lived this passage.

We often look upon a Gospel passage as a past historical event, something we can observe and judge from a distance.

From that standpoint we risk missing the point that the Gospel is a word of power which calls for a personal response. Imaginative contemplation of a Gospel scene moves us from the stance of observer to that of participant.

If we have never prayed Gospel passages in this way, the experience may seem strange at first. However, it gradually becomes easier. Such contemplation of a Gospel scene can be a method of communal as well as individual prayer. When a group is praying the Gospel passage, individuals may want to share the prayers that the passage has evoked.

Gospel accounts can be the house of God. So, too, can events from life. In his book *Sadhana: A Way to God,* Anthony de Mello draws on his extensive experience in conducting retreats to describe other ways in which the imagination can be a guide to prayer. In imagination we can return to scenes where we felt love and joy, experiencing again the positive effects of such love. Or we can visit scenes where we experienced God's goodness and love for us. Such contemplations help us to find God in all the events of our life and put us in touch with forgotten sources of grace and strength. Imagination also enables us to experience the world of possibilities in ways that deepen joy and gratitude for our present gifts. One such contemplation which de Mello suggests restores awareness of the miracle of our bodies.

Before beginning any imaginative contemplation it is necessary to spend a few moments quieting our body and mind, relaxing and centering the self. Awareness of our senses and body, yoga, and deep breathing are aids in this. When you are in a relaxed and quiet state,

> imagine you are in the hospital paralyzed. . . . Imagine that you cannot move a single limb of your body from your neck down. . . . Go through your whole day as a paralyzed person. . . . What do you do all day? . . . What do you

think? . . . What do you feel? . . . How do you keep yourself occupied? . . .

In this state, be aware that you still have your sight. . . . Be
grateful for that. . . . Then become aware that you have
your sense of hearing. . . . Be grateful for that too. . . .
Then become aware that you can still think lucidly . . .
that you can speak and express yourself . . . that you have
the sense of taste which brings you pleasure. . . . Be grateful for each one of these gifts of God. . . . Realize how rich
you are in spite of your paralysis! . . .

Now imagine that after a while you begin to respond to
treatment and it is possible for you to move your neck.
Painfully at first, then with greater ease, you can turn your
head from one side to another . . . a much wider area of
vision is offered to you. You can now look from one end
of the ward to the other without having to have your
whole body moved by someone else. . . . Notice how grateful you feel for this too. . . .

Now come back to your present existence and realize that
you are not paralyzed. Move your fingers gently and
realize there is life and movement in them. Wriggle your
toes . . . move your arms and legs. . . . Say a prayer of
thanksgiving to God over each one of these limbs. . . .[6]

During the silent prayer which follows this exercise many find
themselves praying in thanksgiving for simple gifts which they
have taken for granted, even the ability to wipe away tears.
They also become aware of those to whom they minister, and
pray for those who know the pain of loss and dependency in
its many forms. Since contemplating with the imagination
gradually transforms our images of self and world, the images
and emotions experienced in prayer recur in other settings.

One woman out jogging after this prayer became aware again of the gift of being able to run.

While contemplating parables, psalms, Gospel scenes, and events in our life we discover one quality of prayer of the imagination. God's grace meets us as we dwell in the particular and ordinary, as we live in the house of God. God does not appear directly, but in and through the material world.

Through a Glass Darkly

St. Paul tells his hearers that we see God now through a glass darkly. Later we shall see face to face. The puzzles and silences of the parables remind us that God transcends all of our images; they are testimony to the incomprehensibility of the divine. The dark night of the prayer of the imagination is like the dark night of modern life. It comes as the silence and mystery which pervade ordinary existence, the struggle to believe that, as Nikos Kazantzakis says in *The Greek Passion,*

> ... day and night, slowly, ceaselessly,
> salvation is at work ... in the midst of the
> darkness, is laboring deliverance.[7]

Detachment has always been a dimension of Christian prayer. The parables tell us that such detachment is more than the relinquishing of this or that item of existence. Detachment is the freedom to allow our entire worldview to be turned upside down and our deepest values challenged.

Participation in the parables keeps alive this paradox at the heart of the Gospel message in its many shapes and forms. As poetic metaphors, the parables are not reducible to reason. Their impact is closer to that of a Zen koan, where paradox stands as a constant challenge gradually reaching and transforming levels deeper than reason alone can touch. Many of the proverbs and sayings of Jesus have this same quality.

> For anyone who wants to save his life will lose it; but anyone who loses his life for my sake, and for the sake of the gospel, will save it (Mk 8:35–36).

> This is my body which will be given for you (Lk 22:19).

Those who live in the parables for any length of time, resisting the appeal of simple solutions, know their enigmas: answers that are never given, conclusions that do not fit our expectations, contrasts that overturn ordinary common sense calculations. The parable of the good seed that is ruined by the weeds sown by an enemy forces us to live with the question of evil as it reaches out to mix with the goodness in us and others, just as the roots of the weeds interlace with those of the wheat so that to remove the weeds means uprooting the wheat. The details of the story of the prodigal son juxtapose death and life, losing and finding, rejecting and accepting, gnawing hunger and unmerited feasting. God is found in that unrelieved paradox, in that tension of images. When we live in it we know something of the kingdom. In their use of paradox the parables are like the poetry of St. John of the Cross. In them we discover an experience of God in which darkness is light, ignorance is knowledge, and solitude is companionship.

The contemplation of many Gospel passages keeps alive this sense of paradox. If we really enter into Mary's Magnificat (Lk 1:46–55), we are challenged to hold together the small and the great, the humble woman and God's eschatological reversal.[8] The Magnificat's juxtaposition of contrasting images suggests that great things are hidden in the ordinary: the lowly handmaid is exalted and princes are pulled down from their thrones; the hungry are filled with good things and the rich are sent away empty. Paradoxes such as the Magnificat's contrast between poverty and riches prevent our prayer from becoming self-righteous; they help us resist the tendency to reduce God and the purposes of God to the size of our life and expectations. Instead, we learn to wait in prayer for the depth, surprise, gift, and grace of God. A sense of paradox, of the disproportion between human and divine, also imbues prayer with humor and play. It does this because paradox continually points us beyond ourselves, keeping alive that sense of transcendence essential to both humor and play.

It is the Spirit who teaches us the deeper and fuller meaning of the paradox at the heart of Gospel passages and parables, and of The Parable, Jesus Christ. In washing his disciples' feet, Jesus acts out in parable his coming death on the cross and calls all disciples to contemplation of that parable. But it is the Spirit who will bring to light the meaning of the foot-washing in view of the cross, allowing it to be a vehicle of drawing a disciple ever more deeply into an understanding and living of Jesus' death-resurrection, of the power that is service and the glory that comes through weakness.

Finally, God's shattering of our world can come through the contemplation of images other than those found in the Gospels. The life of Thomas Merton contains a striking example of such a revelation. In December 1968, en route to an international meeting on monastic renewal in Bangkok, Thomas Merton visited Ceylon. He went to Polonnaruwa to see the giant Buddhas and take photographs of them. In his *Asian Journal* Merton describes the experience.

> I am able to approach the Buddhas barefoot and undisturbed, my feet in wet grass, wet sand. The silence of the extraordinary faces. The great smiles. Huge and yet subtle. Filled with every possibility, questioning nothing, knowing everything, rejecting nothing, the peace not of emotional refutation . . . that has seen through every question without trying to discredit anyone or anything—

without refutation—without establishing some other argument. For the doctrinaire, the mind that needs well-established positions, such peace, such silence, can be frightening. I was knocked over with a rush of relief and thankfulness at the *obvious* clarity of the figures. . . . Looking at these figures I was suddenly, almost forcibly, jerked clean out of the habitual, half-tied vision of things, and an inner clearness, clarity, as if exploding, from the rocks themselves, became evident and obvious. . . . I don't know when in my life I have ever had such a sense of beauty and spiritual validity running together in one aesthetic illumination. Surely, with Mahabalipuram and Polonnaruwa my Asian pilgrimage has come clear and purified itself. I mean, I know and I have seen what I was obscurely looking for. I don't know what else remains but I have now seen and have pierced through the surface and have got beyond the shadow and the disguise.[9]

When Merton set out on his Asian journey, he felt that something still eluded him, even though he had completed so much of his inner journey. He hoped to find it in the Asian religious communities. The experience at Polonnaruwa brought a certain sense of completeness; the darkness parted momentarily for Merton during this most important experience of his Asian trip.

Simone Weil had a similar experience of the contemplation of an aesthetic object opening her to the experience of God. While repeating the poem, "Love," by the seventeenth century metaphysical poet George Herbert, she was filled with the divine in an unexpected way. In her words, "Christ himself came down and took possession of me."[10] Up to that point in her life, Simone Weil had never read any mystical works. She describes her experience as an unexpected gift of the presence of God's love.

The experiences of Thomas Merton and Simone Weil

indicate the importance of images at various points in our spiritual journey. We have seen how the imagination in prayer takes us more deeply into the ordinary, where God's coming is often indirect and paradoxical, yet unmistakably God's. Images can also provide a path to greater awareness, centering us on God's presence within us and in creation.

The Lamp and the Light

A sacramental vision of the universe is the basis of the spirituality of the twentieth century mystic and paleontologist Teilhard de Chardin. For Teilhard, the secret of life lies in the capacity to see that we live in a multi-dimensional world. All of reality is charged with a divine presence. Teilhard's favorite symbols capture this faith awareness that all is sacred to the person who knows how to see. He uses the image of a lamp to describe his contemplation of God's presence within. In view of Christ's presence the world itself also takes on fire and light. Faith casts a new light on what we are doing and illumines our existing world. The heart of living in constant prayer, or leading a contemplative life, is living in this actual presence of God. These images of the lamp and the light will guide us in reflecting on the way images focus contemplative awareness on the presence of God and enable us to "pray always."

In *The Divine Milieu* Teilhard describes his turning within to the divine presence that grounds his being.

> I took the lamp and, leaving the zone of everyday occupations and relationships where everything seems clear, I went down into my inmost self, to the deep abyss whence I feel dimly that my power of action emanates.[11]

The Christian tradition provides many images as aids in attentiveness to this divine ground of the self. St. Teresa of Avila

writes that she had a distracted mind and found it hard to
achieve inner silence. She recommends using images to turn to
the God within. Imagine your heart as a garden where Christ
walks, or a palace with God as a brilliant diamond at its center.
See God as a fountain at the center of your self or as a brilliant
sun giving light to your whole being. Imagine that you are a
sponge soaked with the presence of God.[12] A woman living
several centuries before Teresa, Catherine of Siena, also used
a metaphor to preserve awareness of God's presence within
her. Her favorite image was that of the cell. Her letters to her
disciples frequently carry reminders of the cell which we carry
about with us. This is the cell of true knowledge of ourselves.
It is here that we also find awareness of God's love for us.

Through the centuries Christians have discovered visual
and verbal symbols, such as the cross, sun, rose, heart, fire,
light, litanies, and the names of God, to be rich and appropriate guides in dwelling upon our deepest identity and evoking a
presence and a center. Through silent attention and simple
gazing we remain in God's presence. Such contemplation of
images may also be a way of deepening the meaning of biblical
symbols in our life, and it can be combined with various kinds
of movement. The heart of the Gospel message is found in the
image of the seed falling into the ground and dying in order to
bring forth fruit. The image of the seed embodies the paschal
mystery of death and resurrection. We can contemplate this
image by dancing it or by taking a walk with it and seeing the
world through it. The rite of Christian initiation during the
Easter vigil speaks of initiation in terms of such an evangelization of the cosmos. The paschal mystery embraces fire, wind,
wax, bees, light and darkness, water, oil, nakedness, bread,
wine, aromas, words, gestures, and relationships.

Such an evangelization of the cosmos is the final direction
of the use of the imagination in prayer. In such prayer the

world takes on fire and light for us; we celebrate what God is doing everywhere. If we wish to see God, we need to remember how near God is to us: "Emmanuel. God with us." Praying the poetry of the psalms prepares us to see the poetry everywhere. Dwelling in the parables alerts us to the parables of life. Through praying them we come to see that God is present in such seemingly insignificant experiences as reconciliation between fathers and sons, efforts of widows to live on fixed incomes, and refusals to accept an invitation to a wedding. This desire to see God and be united with God in all things has attracted many Christians to the mysticism of Hasidic Judaism. For the Hasidim the presence of God appears in the community's everyday life: in family, business, marriage, social structures. One characteristic of the Hasidic community is *hitlahavut*, the fire of ecstasy. Those who do not learn to experience the fire of ecstasy in their lives are not capable of the joy of paradise when they die. To taste the goodness of God is to anticipate the joy of heaven.[13] As Elie Wiesel writes in *Souls on Fire* of the Baal Shem's message to the Jews: "He taught them to fight sadness with joy. 'The man who looks only at himself cannot but sink into despair, yet as soon as he opens his eyes to the creation around him, he will know joy.' And this joy leads to the absolute, to redemption, to God; that was the new truth as defined by the Baal Shem."[14]

Praying with the imagination not only enkindles this fire of joy that comes from finding God in all of creation. It also nourishes the fire of love. The final test of any form of prayer is whether it leads us to live according to the Gospel pattern of Jesus' life. The First Letter of John tells us that true love for God will bring forth the strongest love for others. We must rely on our living relationship toward others to measure whether we have been truly touching the God of love.

Notes

1. *In Parables. The Challenge of the Historical Jesus.* (New York: Harper & Row, 1973), p. 33.

2. I have in mind here work on the parables by John Dominic Crossan, *In Parables*; Robert Funk, *Language, Hermeneutic and Word of God* (New York: Harper & Row, 1966); Norman Perrin, *Jesus and the Language of the Kingdom* (Philadelphia: Fortress Press, 1976); Pheme Perkins, *Hearing the Parables of Jesus* (New York: Paulist Press, 1981).

3. Quoted by Amos N. Wilder in *Early Christian Rhetoric. The Language of the Gospel* (Cambridge: Harvard U. Press, 1971), p. 71.

4. Sally TeSelle, *Speaking in Parables. A Study in Metaphor and Theology* (Philadelphia: Fortress Press, 1975), pp. 71–72.

5. *The Spiritual Exercises of Saint Ignatius,* trans. Henry Keane, S.J. (London: Burns Oates & Washbourne, 1952), p. 43.

6. Anthony de Mello, S.J., *Sadhana. A Way To God* (St. Louis: The Institute of Jesuit Sources, 1978), pp. 86–87.

7. Trans. Jonathan Griffin (New York: Simon and Schuster, 1964), p. 169.

8. See Robert C. Tannehill, "The Magnificat as Poem," *The Journal of Biblical Literature* 93 (1974), pp. 263–275.

9. *The Asian Journal of Thomas Merton,* ed. Naomi Burton, Brother Patrick Hart, and James Laughlin (New York: New Directions, 1973), pp. 233–236.

10. Simone Weil, *Waiting for God,* trans. Emma Craufurd (New York: Harper & Row, 1973), p. 69.

11. (New York: Harper & Row, 1968), pp. 76–77.

12. *Interior Castle,* trans. E. Allison Peers (New York: Doubleday & Company, 1961).

13. See Martin Buber, *Hasidism* (New York: The Philosophical Library, Inc., 1948).

14. Trans. Marion Wiesel (New York: Vintage Books, 1973), p. 26.

V. Christian Self-Image

We have long known that our self-image is the key to much of our behavior. We act in a certain way because of the way we see ourselves, as worthwhile and loved, or as unlovable and inadequate. Many of us are crippled by negative self-images. Yet, while we have recognized the importance of our self-image, this knowledge has not had the power it might have had in our lives. Although we have referred to our self-image, we have treated it as an idea, capable of being changed by stronger intellectual arguments and a firmer will. We have tried to convince ourselves that we are lovable instead of imagining ourselves as loved. We have carried painful memories without knowing how they can be healed, that is, by reliving the event imaginatively with the Lord. Our attempts at conversion have failed because we have forgotten that our image of self must be healed on the level of the imagination.

This recognition of the power of our self-image, as image, is crucial to the process of Christian growth. Our self-image needs to be healed again and again and brought back into conformity with the image God has of us. God's imagings of us are found in the Bible, beginning with the Book of Genesis.

One of the oldest stories in the Bible portrays God as a potter, molding human clay and breathing life into it. From earth and divine breath the potter creates a human being. With this creation account in the second chapter of Genesis, the

Yahwist answers the questions that lie deepest in every human heart: What am I? Why am I here? Earthborn, but alive with something of God's own spirit, the human person continually transcends self. The person brought to life by the divine potter is an openness to God, a capacity for the infinite.

Next to the Yahwist creation account is another poetic metaphor describing the origins of human life. The Priestly narrative which opens the Book of Genesis also declares that the person is a manifestation of God.

> And God created humankind in his image;
> in the image of God created he him;
> male and female created he them (Gen 1:27).[1]

In an earlier verse the writer refers to the person as the image and likeness of God. The Hebrew word for image, *selem*, is a rare scriptural term. It describes an exact reproduction of the original, like a statue or copy. The Priestly writer modifies its meaning by combining it with the more abstract and vague Hebrew term *demut*, likeness or similarity. Even taken together, however, the terms fail to explain exactly how humankind images the divine. Commentators attempt to describe it in various ways. The divine image is found in human reason; we image God because we are rational. Or this image is a divine spark within the person, a promise of immortality. Others find the divine image in the gift of human freedom, human creativity, or human dominion over all creation. One general line of agreement emerges amid the variety of interpretations. It is the conviction that man and woman are co-creators with God: they share God's responsibility for creation, including the creation of the self.

By declaring that the human person is created in the image of God, the poets of Genesis give us a portrait of our potential selves, of the dignity and value that is meant to be ours. Another poet, T.S. Eliot, describes our fleeting glimpse of this potential self in "Little Giddings" as:

> The voice of the hidden waterfall
> And the children in the apple tree
> Not known, because not looked for
> But heard, half-heard, in the stillness
> Between two waves of the sea.[2]

We do not always act according to this divine image. The Hebrew writers also trace the story of a fallen imagination and the consequences of evil images for the self and the human community. They chronicle the struggle between creative and destructive images, a struggle which occurs at every stage of human development. Their account of the ever widening circle of sin captures the mystery of the human capacity to replace images which strengthen and affirm the life of God with images that weaken and destroy it. The isolated self replaces the communal self. The inadequate self supplants the worthwhile self. In *Markings* Dag Hammarskjold describes this tension of images in his own life.

> To let go of the image which in the eyes of this world bears your name, the image fashioned in your consciousness by social ambition and sheer force of will. To let go and fall, fall—in trust and blind devotion. Towards another, another. . . .[3]

The divine image in the human is not a sure possession. It is rather a capacity to respond to God. The person is changed by degrees into the divine likeness. This is what we mean by Christian growth. The Spirit lives and acts within each person and all of creation, moving them toward transformation into the mystery of Christ, the true image of God.

He is the image of the unseen God
and the firstborn of all creation... (Col 1:15).

In Jesus Christ we discover a new image filled with power in the Spirit to overcome other evil and inadequate images of the self. The healing of our self-image calls for the redemption of the imagination. H. Richard Niebuhr emphasizes that "the errors and superstitions fostered by bad imagination in this realm cannot be overcome by eliminating ideas of self and of value for selves, but only by more adequate images of the same order."[4] It is not enough to reason or will a new self. The development of a Christian self-image is the work of the imagination in response to the Spirit.

Christian growth, seen in terms of the imagination, has three dimensions: (1) attention to images as revealing the self, especially in its deeper aspects, (2) the healing and transformation of inadequate or destructive images of self, and (3) the discernment and following of God's call in our life story. The Spirit is at work in all of these processes since they are part of our maturing into the fullness of the image of Christ.

Who Am I? Images as Insight

We all spend a large part of our lives trying to know and understand ourselves. Sages in every culture teach us that such knowledge is the beginning of wisdom. Yet a clear grasp of the singular particularity which is our self usually eludes us. Alfred North Whitehead speaks to this dilemma when he reminds us that where the deeper truths of life are concerned, language halts behind intuition and insight. We know more than we can say. It is always poetry rather than philosophy which comes closest to capturing some of these inexpressible depths. In his book *Metaphors of Self: The Meaning of Autobiog-*

raphy, James Olney says the same thing about the pursuit of self-knowledge.

> One cannot . . . hope to capture with a straight-on look, or expect to transmit directly to another, one's own sense of self; at most one may be able to discover a similitude, a metaphor, for the feeling of selfhood.[5]

The self is known and shared only in indirect ways.

Because insight into the self comes initially in the poetry of the imagination, reflection on our Christian existence or the sharing of our life of faith with others requires close attention to the images that arise in us. There are three stages in such attention. First we welcome our images into awareness. Since they are often largely unconscious, we may be aware of them at first only as an emotion or as a vague hunch or intuition. It takes courage to search out the image behind the emotion. In the second stage, we need to linger with the image for a time, allowing it to play out its insight. In the final stage we attempt to express the insight we have gained and incorporate it into our life. A closer look at each stage will help to clarify this process.

In one of his last entries for the years 1941–42, Dag Hammarskjold writes in *Markings:* "But only through the self-knowledge we gain by pursuing the fleeting light in the depth of our being do we reach the point where we can grasp what faith is."[6] Since images are closer to bodily existence than concepts, the fleeting light first appears to the inner eye of the imagination. To capture these glimpses of self we need to record our dreams or explore the images we discover in waking consciousness. Behind attitudes of discouragement and confusion, or emotions of fear, depression, and resentment are the images responsible for these attitudes and emotions. Spiritual direction is one means of eliciting these images. For example, one young woman considering a change in vocation described her present existence as a root-bound plant which no longer bloomed and was beginning to wither. Another woman enmeshed in a job conflict saw herself at the bottom of a pit with people hurling objects at her from above. A young man having difficulty talking about his father's recent death said the image that came to him was of two trees that had grown side by side for many years so that their roots beneath the soil were intricately intertwined with one another. These roots were now being violently ripped apart.

Once an image presents itself, it is important to linger with it for a time, to play with it until it has delivered its entire message. Hans-Georg Gadamer describes play in *Truth and Method* as always involving something

> with which the player plays, and which automatically responds to his move with a countermove. Thus the cat at play chooses the ball of wool because it responds to play, and ball games will be with us forever because the ball is freely mobile in every direction, appearing to do surprising things of its own accord.[7]

Such surprises also occur when we play with an image in our life. It will amplify itself, making its own connections with different aspects of our life. Exploring her image of a root-bound plant, the young woman realized that the air, water, and light which had nourished the plant were now also cut off. She had let ritual, prayer, and a faith community drop from her life. The young man describing the image of his father's death listened to the feeling accompanying the tearing apart of the roots. He felt it as a deep pulsing pain at the heart of the earth and recognized that he carried that pain within him. In working with dreams as images, the Jungian psychologist James Hillman stresses the importance of reading and rereading, hearing and rehearing, an image. In other words, we are to befriend it. Hillman follows Jung in believing that as the shape of an image emerges, so does its meaning. As Jung wrote:

> Image and meaning are identical; and as the first takes shape, the latter becomes clear. Actually, the pattern needs no interpretation: it portrays its own meaning.[8]

Contemplation of images is a way of asking them to teach us. As we interact with an image, we discover insights which lead to greater wholeness in the spiritual life.

Finally, we verify the insights that come from the imagination by incorporating them into our life. Exploring images should lead us to the kind of self-understanding and self-acceptance which is the foundation of Christian growth. As the images reveal their insights, they help us see more clearly what paths of action we are called to follow: the strengthening of a life of prayer, greater trust in God, a choice of a ministry for social justice, or changes in our relationships with family and friends.

Along with such insights there is often a strong realization that many of our images stand in need of healing and transformation. They are blocking rather than enabling Christian growth and action. New images must replace the old. In Christ such transforming images are revealed to us. They are the key to that conversion of heart which is the Gospel's central demand.

Create a New Heart in Me

When we listen closely to the images which reveal us to ourselves, we often become aware of a problem. We may realize a need for self-acceptance, the courage to embrace with more love a self that is fearful and timid in the face of life's challenge, a self that is limited and unable to be or to achieve all that we would like, a self that has not always been loved well, or a self that is sexual in ways never fully integrated. We see the need to pass from one image to another, to die to an image of self as totally independent and not in need of anyone, a self that is unforgiving and incapable of loving someone again after a hurt, or a self that is jealous and possessive, incapable of allowing others to be free. We need to die to these images and be reborn to a self more like Christ. Paul writes to the Corinthians: "And for anyone who is in Christ, there is a new creation; the old creation has gone, and now the new one is here" (2 Cor 5:17–18). This is the new heart which Ezekiel promises when God replaces hearts of stone with hearts of flesh (Ez 36:26).

Conversion is a gradual process of turning toward God. It is the discovery of those images by which we are called to understand ourselves. This movement is mediated by Christ who is both the self-revelation of God and the ultimate key to understanding our existence. Bernard Lonergan describes revelation as "God's entry into man's making of man."[9] Conversion is not a sudden event. It is a continual process of large and small conversions by which the Spirit, the power of the new creation, brings us by degrees into a fuller image of Christ. We share best in this creative process when we understand how personal change comes about.

Recent right-brain research and its application by different groups of therapists can help us here. During the 1950's, the work of Joseph Kamiya and other researchers at San Francisco's Langley Porter Clinic resulted in an hypothesis that there are two modes of consciousness corresponding to the two hemispheres of the brain. The left hemisphere of the brain, which is connected to the right side of the body, makes possible those modes of consciousness which are primarily analytical, conceptual, and linear. Its approach to change is through logic and reasoning. The mode of consciousness made possible by the right hemisphere of the brain, which is connected to the left side of the body, is more intuitive, imaginative, mythical, visual, and associative. Change in this mode of consciousness requires metaphoric communication: image, metaphor, paradox, humor, ritual, myth.

Since Christian growth demands conversion of heart, it cannot neglect insights into the dynamics of change such as those provided by right-brain research. Conversion requires more than the reception of new information. We may fully understand conceptually that God loves us but be unable to bring our actions into line with that knowledge. Or we may have gone over the reasons why we must seek reconciliation in a relationship again and again, but still not be able to do so. Resources for growth are seriously limited when the language of the right brain is undervalued. Paul Watzlawick deplores this loss in his discussion of *The Language of Change,* speaking here specifically of ritual.

> Ritual has largely been forced into the underground and thus has greatly restricted the contribution of the right hemisphere to the solution of concrete problems, or else (ritual) threatens the reasonable order of the world by the dark, orphic violence which is typical of the repressed.[10]

Watzlawick gives many illustrations of the power of right-brain language patterns to bring about change, including in this language the joke, the rhyme, dreams, aphorisms, puns, and allusions. Such language evokes rather than explains. The work of Watzlawick and others has revived awareness of the power of right-brain communication in human change.

In *Getting Well Again,* O. Carl Simonton and Stephanie Matthews-Simonton chronicle their use of positive mental images in the treatment of cancer patients.[11] Patients are systematically trained to use specific exercises in visual concentration. They create visualizations which to them personally represent both their illness and the conquering of their illness. Cancer cells may be represented as weak and poorly armed knights. The white blood cells are envisioned as powerful well-equipped knights on charging steeds, bearing down on the cancer cells and killing them off. Repetition of this visualization several times a day has been found very effective in bringing about the remission of cancer. The method can be used on many other types of human problems as well. Douglas Anderson, in *New Approaches to Family Pastoral Care,* integrates the Christian tradition with the therapeutic power of communicating with the metaphoric mind. He argues that each family has a guiding image or metaphor by which family members understand and respond to the world.[12] These metaphors, such as family as team, or family as poor, or family as backward, can either block or enable change. The continuing transformation of a family's metaphor is essential to helping them change, and it is the Spirit who guides the family into a new metaphor.

What therapy has discovered as the power of right-brain communication is already a central element in biblical literature. Scripture contains central images and an account of the community's application of these images to its life. Its language, as we have seen, is not speculative and abstract. Rather, the Bible is filled with stories, images, paradigms, pictures, and vignettes. One aspect of openness to the Spirit's transforming power is letting Scripture's images challenge the images we have held until the biblical images gradually become dominant in our lives. Christian growth occurs as we apply such images as Suffering Servant, kingdom of God, Son of Man, covenant, and communion to our self-understanding and our life circumstances. This conviction is central to James McClendon's treatment of *Biography as Theology,* and he illustrates it from the lives of Dag Hammarskjold and Martin Luther King.

> Hammarskjold understands himself as Christ's brother, as brother to the Brother; he sees the point of his life as a sacrifice to be offered; life is lived in the confidence that the unheard of is at the limits of reality, and later God is invoked under a triune image—Father, Brother, Spirit. King understands his work under the image of the Exodus; he is leading his people on a new crossing of the Red Sea; he is a Moses who goes to the mountaintop, but who is not privileged to enter with his people into the promised land.[13]

McClendon stresses that such images are not peripheral to faith, but that people live their very lives out of them.

Conversion of heart sometimes calls for the healing of resentments, hurts, and fears that are blocking growth and joy. Perhaps someone has hurt us badly and the hurt is still alive within us. Or we fear failure and rejection and shrink back from new encounters and projects. What we need to do is go back to the original scene that hurt or frightened us, bringing the Lord with us. Anthony de Mello suggests one possible way of doing this in *Sadhana.*

> Return to some scene in the past where you have felt pain or grief or hurt or fear or bitterness. . . . Relive the event. . . . But this time seek and find the presence of the Lord in it. . . . In what way is he present there? . . .
>
> Or, imagine that the Lord himself is taking part in the event. . . . What role is he playing? . . . Speak to him. Ask him the meaning of what is happening. . . . Listen to what he says in reply. . . .[14]

The healing of negative images often requires returning to the scene several times in imagination in this way.

Contrast and convergence between different images also brings about imaginative shock and leads to the renewal and healing of images. A way of opening our imagination to grace is to move back and forth between contrasting images, our own image which needs healing, and a New Testament image which is its healing, e.g., a scene of our resentment or unwillingness to forgive, and an image of Christ on the cross forgiving his enemies (Lk 23:33–34); an image of ourselves as unlovable and lacking potential, and a scene where Jesus affirms an outcast who is small of stature (Lk 19:1–10) or a sinful woman who is well known (Lk 7:36–50). We must return to the new image again and again until it begins to transform our inadequate image of self.

Sometimes it is not the individual but the Christian community itself which clings to distorted images. Then the imagination at the heart of a tradition must be healed. This frees the Spirit to draw the tradition closer to the new creation. Such healing is now occurring through images of women in the Jewish and Christian traditions. As with destructive self-images, here too a negative critique of the tradition is not enough. Positive images must replace faulty ones. This is slowly happening. We now recognize Genesis 1:27 as an account of male and female created in equality, freedom, and uniqueness, both together reflecting the image of God.

> And God created humankind in his image;
> in the image of God he created him;
> male and female he created them.

We are discovering new images of women in Martha, Mary Magdalene and the Samaritan woman, each of whom receives Jesus' revelation of himself as Messiah or Risen One and goes as disciple to bear witness to him. Emerging from the tradition are women deacons like Phoebe (Rom 16:1), women prophets like Anna and Elizabeth (Lk 2:36–38; 1:41–45), and women teachers like Priscilla (Acts 18:26). The discovery of such positive images continues and is crucial to woman's relationship to herself, the community, and God.

Imagination enters into Christian growth, then, in the two ways we have described. Images bring insight into the deepest levels of our self. When our images are inadequate or destructive, healing and transformation takes place through the work of the imagination as the Spirit leads us into more adequate images of the self. Linked to these is a third way in which the imagination functions in Christian growth. Through the imagination we relive our life story, the narrative that links our images through time. Individual images can be fully understood only when they are woven into the texture of a life. Further, it is only in terms of our life story that we can apply the final criterion of Christian conversion: How open are we to the call or will of God in our life?

Life Story and God's Will

The Yahwist account of creation which we recalled in opening this chapter describes the human person as alive with God's own spirit. Christian growth is ever greater openness to this presence of God in one's life. Gerard Manley Hopkins describes this continual seeking after God in the first lines of "The Wreck of the Deutschland":

> Thou mastering me
> God! giver of breath and bread;
> World's strand, sway of the sea;
> Lord of living and dead;
> Thou hast bound bones and veins in me, fastened me flesh,

And after it almost unmade, what with dread,
Thy doing: and dost thou touch me afresh?
Over again I feel thy finger and find thee.[15]

Several questions cluster around this effort to find God in our life: How do I know that it is God's spirit which is leading me? Where do I look for the call of God? What is the relationship between human well-being and God's will? The use of one's life story in the search for God's will provides new insight into many of these questions.

One of the classic examples of finding God in the details and patterns of a life story is the *Confessions* of St. Augustine. The *Confessions* is a conversation with God. Augustine is convinced that the events of his life are God's revelation to him, and his prayer is a recollection of himself before God. This man's spiritual odyssey is the story of Everyone, the paradigm of all who search through time to find the image-stream of their life before God. Augustine's *Confessions* is a story of experience, but of experience as opening one to the call which God addresses to the self. The existential details, the moments and situations of Augustine's life such as his involvement with Manichaeism, skepticism, and Neo-Platonism, manifest the eternal call of God in his life: "Deep within me I recognized the working of your will and I praised your name, rejoicing in my faith" (IX.4). Such recollection draws Augustine into communication with God. It also takes him back to the beginning of all time, to Genesis. There Augustine discovers a deepened sense of his contingency which opens him to the presence of God as creative power.

In *Metaphors of Self,* James Olney terms an autobiography like the *Confessions* a form of symbolic memory.[16] Imagination is a necessary element of true recollection. By means of it a person reconstructs past experience and is able to give a verdict on his or her self and life. A life story is a poetic metaphor that enables us to span the distance between our past and present self, between the self that is already formed and the self that is becoming. Imaginative recollection also prepares us to hear the call of God and increase our openness to the purpose of God in our life. Some insights from the contemporary movement of process theology, based on the thought of Alfred North Whitehead, are helpful in seeing how this is so.

Whitehead speaks of God in the world as "the perpetual vision of the road which leads to the deeper realities."[17] Following God's will means openness to a direction, to a fullness of possibility, but not a certainty regarding the specific action which is best at each moment of our becoming. The purpose of God does not destroy a person's capacity to love and choose freely; it is not the unveiling of an already determined story. God's will is a direction revealed gradually in relation to where we are at each point in our life. God takes into account our past failures and successes, our present circumstances, relationships, weaknesses and strengths, and offers us possibilities and ideals to direct our actions. Whitehead describes God as "the poet of the world, gently leading us forward by his vision of truth, beauty, and goodness."[18] God's purpose is a call to move forward out of the past into the possibilities of the future. In *Markings* Dag Hammarskjold sees Jesus as someone who followed such a road of possibility to the end.

He had assented to a possibility in his being, of which he had had his first inkling when he returned from the desert. If God required anything of him, he would not fail. Only recently, he thought, had he begun to see more clearly, and to realize that the road of possibility might lead to the cross. He knew, though, that he had to follow it, still uncertain as to whether he was indeed "the one who shall

bring it to pass," but certain that the answer could only be
learned by following the road to the end. The end *might*
be a death without significance—as well as being the end
of the road of possibility.[19]

God's aim or call is different for each individual, and life
stories open us to this direction of God in several ways.

The first way in which our life story opens us to God's
purpose is in terms of memory. Memory is the basis of hope.
The stories of the past reveal to us the positive possibilities of
the present. God's call takes account of where we are and
always invites us to further growth. In following that call,
then, we need to know who we have become. For it is the self
we are now which is the basis of a realistic decision regarding
future options. A path too safe, with no risk, means a loss of
opportunities for growth. A path too wild or dangerous is not
in keeping with the circumstances and conditions of the self.
Recollection of the values of the past through the telling of
our story opens us to the possible, which is where God's
direction is found. It also gives us strength to choose these
possibilities. As was the case with Augustine, so too our memories reveal God present in times of suffering and sin, mercy
and joy. Like St. Paul who describes his brush with shipwreck,
danger, near death, and discouragement, we find in past experiences of God's faithfulness the courage we need to embrace
new risks.

Our life story helps us discern God's purpose in a second
way by revealing in retrospect the patterns of our life. In
telling our story we do not simply relate one episode after
another: an accident, a friendship, a job, a move. Rather, what
Paul Ricoeur describes is more frequently the case: "To tell
and to follow a story is already to *reflect upon* events in order to
encompass them in successive wholes."[20] When we recollect
our life, sequence and pattern appear; this ordering is already

an act of judgment on our life. The pattern we find may be one of greater freedom, outreach, and concern for others. Or it may be a story of increasing isolation and self-preoccupation. Life orientations come clear only in retrospect. T.S. Eliot reflects in "The Dry Salvages":

> We had the experience but missed the meaning,
> And approach to the meaning restores the experience
> In a different form. . . .[21]

As with any story, there are discoveries, revelations, and surprises in the telling: gifts of grace now forgotten, wounds not yet healed, goals and desires persisting over many years.

Where is God in all of this? Some see God's will as a detailed plan for one's life. The task is to discover the actions which best fit this divine blueprint; if we do not, we have failed to fulfill God's will for us. Whitehead, on the other hand, sees the purpose of God as very broad, able to be fulfilled in many different ways. The divine call is to life in ever greater harmony with ourselves and with our entire environment. God is "the mirror which discloses to every creature its own greatness."[22] God's purpose is compassion and reverence for all of life. Since this purpose is a direction and continuing call, the extent of our growth in sensitivity, justice, humanity, and wholeness will only be fully seen at the end. Monica Furlong illustrates this in her recent biography of Thomas Merton.

> As the years stripped away the obvious answers and the comforting illusions, he felt he was left with little but his humanity. Like Dietrich Bonhoeffer in his Nazi prison, he began to see that the highest spiritual development was to be "ordinary," to be fully a man, in the way few human

beings succeed in becoming so simply and naturally themselves . . . the "measure" of what others might be if society
did not distort them with greed or ambition or lust or
desperate want.[23]

Along the way our story is always "to be continued." No
sooner do we arrive than the Spirit calls us to be moving again.
As Merton's story shows, this journey is toward our deepest
selves.

The search for God's purpose in our life is a journey of
uncertainty. There is no way of saying beyond any doubt that
our actions conform with God's will. Our life story reveals that
we frustrate and incompletely attain the possibilities God
offers us. The narrative of our life sometimes manifests God's
presence only obscurely. What we see is usually only a mo-
mentary light. But we need to trust the hunches and guesses
that come to us in an attitude of openness and love. This
openness prepares the way for greater divine presence in our
life and ever closer movement toward God's vision of what we
might become. It is the essential attitude found in the Gospel
portrayal of Jesus and Mary, a readiness to pray what T.S.
Eliot in "The Dry Salvages" calls the "hardly, barely prayable
prayer of the one Annunciation."[24]

Other people are a vital guide in testing the spirits and
finding the path of the Spirit of God. That is why Christians
share their stories of faith. The patterns and direction of our
life are often clearer to someone else than they are to us. This
is especially the case when we are involved in the struggle and
agony of decision making. Telling our story to someone who
listens in love and offers some feedback brings insight, hope,
and a release from loneliness. Dorothy Day concludes her
autobiography *The Long Loneliness* with some reflections on
how significant love in community was in the development of

the Catholic Worker Movement: "We cannot love God unless we love each other, and to love we must know each other."[25] Shared stories generate the courage and insight necessary to follow the demands of that love.

Hearing the stories of others is as important as telling our own story. Such stories are channels of grace. They too embody the call of God and fire our imaginations with possibilities for ourselves. Since we live out of our imaginations, we cannot live in a certain way or see ourselves as the people we want to be until we see that wished-for life and self in our imagination. The story of the "little way" of Thérèse of Lisieux gripped the imagination of Mother Teresa of Calcutta. By doing what she could do in her particular set of nineteenth-century circumstances with love of God and purity of intention, Thérèse revealed the primacy of the ordinary. Her story moved Mother Teresa to live out a similar vision on the streets of India. The life of the sixteenth-century mystic and reformer Teresa of Avila led to the conversion to Catholicism of the brilliant twentieth-century German philosopher Edith Stein. Whether they come from the past or the present such stories define specifically what living out the will of God might mean and they stimulate our imaginations with possibilities.

Such stories, circumscribed as they are by a particular set of individual and historical conditions, illustrate what was said earlier about the call of God. It comes to us in terms of our actual situation. Whitehead believes that limitation is the key to the actual; it is only when the possibilities of life are limited that they can exist at all. Understanding God's purpose in this way provides an antidote against the search for some false and abstract image of self which bears no relationship to our real existence. In its love of the limited, the Christian story is, in fact, a comic form of remembrance. The comic vision of life affirms our inescapable humanity and the limitations of our creatureliness. William Lynch describes the function of the comic imagination to be

> a perpetual and funny, if disconcerting, reminder that it is the limited concrete which is the path to insight and salvation. Its whole art is to be an art of anamnesis, or memory, of the bloody human (in the sense in which the English use that adjective) as a path to God, or to any form of the great.[26]

The Christian story is a comedy since in Christ it shows us the inescapable link between God and our humanity. It also adds resurrection to the potentially tragic experiences of struggle and death. With resurrection the Spirit's work of bringing us to the fullness of the image of Christ is complete.

We have seen what an important role the imagination holds in our transformation into this image of Christ. We must be converted, not only on the level of concepts and ideas, but at the deeper level of our self-image. This process includes the insights which come through the discovery of the important images in our life, the healing and conversion of these images in response to the Spirit, and the linking of these images into a story of openness to God's purpose in our life. Only as we continue to tell that story do we gradually discover what it means to be created in the divine image.

Notes

1. For a discussion of this translation, see Phyllis Trible, *God and the Rhetoric of Sexuality* (Philadelphia: Fortress Press, 1978), pp. 12 ff.

2. In *The Complete Poems and Plays. 1909–1950* (New York: Harcourt, Brace & World, Inc., 1952), p. 145.

3. Trans. Leif Sjoberg and W.H. Auden (New York: Alfred A. Knopf, 1974), p. 24.

4. *The Meaning of Revelation* (New York: Macmillan Company, Inc., 1941), p. 79.

5. (Princeton: University Press, 1972), pp. 266–267.

6. P. 16.

7. (New York: Seabury Press, 1975), p. 95.

8. *The Collected Works of C.G. Jung* (Bollingen Series 20), ed. Gerhard Adler, Michael Fordham, and Herbert Read. Trans. R.F.C. Hull (Princeton: University Press, 1953ff), Vol. 8 #402.

9. Bernard Lonergan, S.J., *A Second Collection,* ed. William F. J. Ryan, S.J. and Bernard J. Tyrrell, S.J. (Philadelphia: The Westminster Press, 1974), p. 62.

10. (New York: Basic Books, Inc., 1978), p. 155.

11. (New York: Bantam Books, Inc., 1980).

12. (Philadelphia: Fortress Press, 1980).

13. (New York: Abingdon Press, 1974), p. 93.

14. *Sadhana: A Way to God* (St. Louis: The Institute of Jesuit Sources, 1978), p. 68.

15. *Gerard Manley Hopkins: Poems and Prose,* ed. W.H. Gardner (Baltimore: Penguin Books, 1953), p. 12.

16. P. 37. Olney is applying the philosophy of Ernst Cassirer here.

17. *Religion in the Making* (Cleveland: World Publishing Co., 1960), p. 151.

18. *Process and Reality* (New York: The Macmillan Co., 1969), p. 408.

19. P. 68.

20. "The Narrative Function." In *The Poetics of Faith. Essays Offered to Amos Niven Wilder, Part 2, Semeia* 13, ed. William A. Beardslee (The Society of Biblical Literature, 1978), p. 185.

21. *The Complete Poems and Plays,* p. 133.

22. *Religion in the Making,* p. 148.

23. *Merton: A Biography* (San Francisco: Harper & Row, 1980), p. xviii.

24. In *The Complete Poems and Plays,* p. 132.

25. (New York: Image Books, 1959), p. 276.

26. "Theology and the Imagination III. The Problem of Comedy," *Thought* 30 (Spring 1955), 23.

VI. Images of God

Several decades ago in *Your God Is Too Small*
J.B. Phillips demonstrated the destructive power of inadequate
images of God.[1] His list of images included God as Resident
Policeman, Parental Hangover, Managing Director, Grand
Old Man, and God-In-A-Box. Most had no quarrel with
Phillips' selection of images. We all found traces of them in
our experience, and their inadequacy seemed obvious. Phil-
lips' recommendation for overcoming the limitations of these
images also seemed sound: turn to the God revealed in Jesus
Christ.

The situation today is even more complex. Now the
concern is not only the images of God we form in ignorance of
Scripture. The names of God within the Judaeo-Christian
tradition itself are a problem. Male metaphors predominate:
Judge, King, Lord, Master, Father. Faced with the dominance
of this patriarchal language for God, some have looked outside
the tradition for imagery of God in the experience of nature or
in goddess-worshiping cultures. Others see the solution in
better explanations of the traditional metaphors. As Robert
Hammerton-Kelly writes in *God the Father: Theology and Pa-
triarchy in the Teaching of Jesus:* "God the Father symbolizes
grace and freedom, maturity and faith, intimacy with the
divine source of life, a confidence in the final goodness of
existence, the possibility of growth and creativity."[2] These
meanings are, he contends, the opposite of what the radical

feminists understand by the biblical symbol of Father.

New explanations of patriarchal symbols do not satisfy those who believe that solutions lie not just in new ideas, but more fundamentally in the language of the imagination itself. Images and symbols shape experience on levels deeper than explanations. They survive in the imagination, and it is there that they must be transformed. Subsequent explanations do not undo the more potent work already done by the symbol itself.

One resource for such renewal is traditional strands of imagination, long lost to view, which refer to God in feminine imagery. Reclaiming these aspects of the tradition is not of concern just to women. Our images of God affect all men's and women's possibilities for existence and shape the way they understand their call to holiness. Besides, the full significance of any individual metaphor for God can be understood only in relation to the complete range of names for God. It is a wealth of divine images which most forcefully reminds us that God is not found in any single image but transcends them all. Too much imagination is not, as some have feared in the past, the greatest threat to the otherness of God. It is rather poverty of imagination which limits our understanding of both human holiness and divine transcendence. We will look more closely at each of these issues in the rest of this chapter, dividing them into three sections: (1) divine image and human possibility; (2) polyphony: the many sounds of God's name; (3) the idol and the image. Some final reflections will show how process theology's portrayals of God as Poet, Great Companion, and Final Wisdom are a promising contemporary imagery for God.

Divine Image and Human Possibility

Unless we see the importance which images of God have in our life, there is little point in substituting new ones for old.

It is therefore worthwhile to review briefly what is at stake in our way of speaking about God.

Images of God are more fundamental to our life of faith than ideas or concepts. This is a point stressed by John Henry Newman, the nineteenth century Anglican convert to Roman Catholicism. In his *Grammar of Assent,* Newman explores the forces that account for the strength or weakness of our religious beliefs. Belief in God, he says, originates in our imagination. Our conviction that God is personal and good, Lord and Judge, comes to us as an image, not an abstract notion or idea. This image results from pleasant or painful experiences of conscience: self-approval, hope, sorrow, fear. These initial experiences are the basis of a real assent to God, which revelation later clarifies and strengthens. Our doctrines of God grow out of our images as we reflect and meditate on their meaning. According to Newman we can either let these images which develop early in life lose their immediacy and vividness so that they become merely intellectual notions, or "the image of God, if duly cherished, may expand, deepen, and be completed."[3] This process of deepening takes place through further internal and external experiences which come in the course of life. Since it is these images which give us a living hold on the truths of faith, they strongly influence our commitments and behavior.

Divine imagery also controls how we relate to God personally. On one level this is rather obvious. The metaphors we use for God allow us to suggest a similarity between something we know concretely, such as a human father, and a reality more obscurely known, God as Father. The biblical stories of God show us the similarities and differences between God and human fathers, thus giving us a context for understanding the metaphor. But this process of comparison between human and divine realities is not mainly a clear-cut rational enterprise. As Philip Wheelwright points out in his discussion of metaphor, such language has shaded edges of meaning. It evokes emotions and attitudes in subtle, rich, and ambiguous ways.[4] All these levels of the meaning of a metaphor such as father influence how we relate to God as Father, for example, in fear or in trust. Further, we are not speculatively comparing two realities which we already know. Imaginative language works by participation. A personal grasp of the imagery comes from entry into a relationship, with the resultant discovery of new possibilities for ourselves. We discover what it is for God to be Spouse or Savior for us only as we actually enter into a relationship with God as revealed in that image.

Medieval spirituality illustrates the fruitfulness of this last point. A number of writers have noted that the spiritual writers of the twelfth through fifteenth centuries spoke of God in symbols reflecting a broader range of human experience than is the case today. Men, as well as women, describe their encounter with the holy in maternal imagery. God is both loving and mighty, mother and father. The Benedictine, Anselm of Canterbury, composed the following prayer:

> But thou also, Jesus, good Lord, art thou not also Mother? Art thou not Mother who art like a hen which gathers her chicks under her wings? Truly, Lord, thou art also Mother. For what others have labored with and brought forth, they have received from thee. Thou first, for their sake and for those they bring forth, in labor went dead, and by dying hast brought forth. . . .[5]

This greater range of divine images opened a wider sphere of human possibilities to both men and women. It supported their dignity and equality.

While women in the Middle Ages did not participate in the authority of the Church on an equal basis with men, they shared equally in the power of holiness. They enriched medieval spirituality through accounts of their own religious experience and writings on the spiritual life. The lives of Christina of Markyate and Catherine of Siena are two examples of this influence. Perhaps best known today is the contribution of a mystic and spiritual director who lived in the last half of the fourteenth century. Julian of Norwich's *Revelations of Divine Love* record her experience of God along with her reflections on that experience. She writes:

> ... and the second person of the Trinity is our Mother in nature in our substantial creation, in whom we are founded and rooted, and he is our Mother of mercy in taking our sensuality. And so our Mother is working on us in various ways, in whom our parts are kept undivided; for in our Mother Christ we profit and increase, and in mercy he reforms and restores us, and by the power of his Passion, his death and his Resurrection he unites us to our substance. So our Mother works in mercy on all his beloved children who are docile and obedient to him. . . .[6]

Christ is the center of Julian's spirituality, but she uses mothering metaphors to describe her experience of both God and Jesus. This medieval ability to keep alive both male and female metaphors for God keeps it clear that God transcends all sexuality and gives equal dignity to the holiness and the experience of both men and women.

The medieval experience highlights a function of divine imagery which we recognize in our historical period as well. Many images of God are socially shared symbols that unite and motivate a community. They inspire our loves and hates, and are the basis for establishing and maintaining positions of authority. The prophet Hosea very effectively used an image of God as Faithful Lover to bring Israel to a realization of her infidelity. The power of symbols can also do damage. Consistently viewing God as Unchanging Absolute may justify maintaining the status quo, whatever it is. Imaging God as male may legitimate woman's subordination in Church and world. The predominance of masculine images of God in the Hebrew Scriptures supports its patriarchal, male-oriented society. Recent arguments against the ordination of women also rely on such support. In October 1971, Rt. Rev. C. Kilmer Myers, Episcopal bishop of California, wrote: "A priest is a 'god symbol' whether he likes it or not. In the imagery of both Old and New Testaments God is represented in masculine imagery."[7] Myers acknowledges that the biblical language is analogous, but he insists that the male image of God pertains to the divine initiative in creation and makes initiative a male rather than female attribute. Since priesthood is a generative, initiating, and giving function, it is a masculine role.

Thus our metaphors of God are central not only to our relationship with God in prayer and worship, but also to our sense of personal and communal possibilities. We must speak of God in human language. It is the only speech we have. Yet we know that God surpasses our language. The Sinai decalogue includes a prohibition against making carved images or likenesses of God (Ex 20:3–6). The account of the revelation of the divine name in Moses' encounter with the burning bush (Ex 3:13–15) reminds us that God is finally unnamable. Within the logic of the imagination there are safeguards which prevent us from mistaking any single metaphor for the literal name of God. If we keep alive a diverse store of images, including both masculine and feminine elements, these names of God enrich and qualify one another, pointing through their interaction to the transcendence of God. In the next two sections we will see how this is so.

Polyphony: The Many Sounds of God's Name

In several of the letters written from his Tegel prison cell in the spring of 1944, Dietrich Bonhoeffer pursues what he calls the image of the polyphony of life. Bonhoeffer's love of music has already been apparent in earlier letters; here he turns to polyphony in music to describe the way our love of God and earthly loves can be united. Love of god, he believes, provides a *cantus firmus* to which the other melodies of life provide a counterpoint. Loving God with our whole hearts need not weaken or injure our earthly loves; we can rejoice with those who rejoice, weep with those who weep, and be anxious with those who are anxious. Christianity puts us in many dimensions of life at once: "Life isn't pushed back into a single dimension, but is kept multi-dimensional and polyphonous."[8] If our faith is to be rich and full, then, we must give up our one-track thinking.

Bonhoeffer's concern that faith be kept multi-dimensional applies especially to our belief in God. Polyphony prevents us from identifying one image with the reality of God. A proper diversity, as Paul Ricoeur notes, is kept alive in the biblical writings through many kinds of discourse.

> Thus God is named in diverse ways in narration that recounts his acts, prophecy that speaks in the divine name, prescription that designates God as the source of the imperative, wisdom that seeks God as the meaning of meaning, and the hymn that invokes God in the second person.[9]

Metaphors personal and impersonal, masculine and feminine, gentle and stern are all combined to reveal something of the Mystery. Nor do these partial names of God simply stand in juxtaposition. They interact with one another and in that interaction enrich the significance of each metaphor: King, Father, Mother, Husband, Rock, Redeemer, and Suffering Servant. Each one has power to evoke the whole network of metaphors and to suggest the many ways that God is with humanity.

We are immediately familiar with one way in which the multiple names of God in the tradition qualify one another. The biblical writings, especially the psalms, use impersonal as well as personal metaphors for God. These impersonal metaphors expand our notions of God and prevent us from identifying God with our image of a person. God is a Shield (Ps 7:10), a Rock, Fortress, Horn of Salvation (Ps 18:2), and a Lamp (Ps 18:28). A favorite image is that of God's protecting wings: "Hide me in the shadow of your wings" (Ps 17:8); we "take shelter in the shadow of your wings" (Ps 36:7).

Impersonal images are also a major motif in the writings of Christian mystics. As with the impersonal metaphors in the biblical tradition, these images expand our approach to the divine Mystery. They testify that the experience of union with God transcends our usual subject/object distinctions. St. Catherine of Siena describes the divine presence as a "ray of love," a "ray of darkness," or the "sea pacific." Marie of the Incarnation, a seventeenth century French mystic, refers to the divine as a "ray of sunlight" which is not seen itself but is the light in which all other things are seen. For her, God is like a great ocean which covers, inundates, and surrounds her completely. Mechthild of Magdeburg describes God as a flame or river of fire which fills the universe. The German mystics refer to the "incomprehensible desert" which is both "ineffable darkness" and "essential light."[10] At times the tradition has experienced tension in relating these impersonal images to the personal metaphors of the Bible. Nonetheless, they continue to be a source of new understandings of our relationship to the divine.

We are rediscovering another strand of traditional imagery for God: God is named in feminine as well as masculine terms.[11] This is especially true of the prophetic tradition, where God is portrayed in parent imagery, as mother as well as father. In some of his most moving poetry, the eighth century prophet Hosea describes God as a loving parent, providing the detailed care that would be the task of a mother in Hebrew society.

> When Israel was a child, I loved him, and I called my son out of Egypt. . . . I myself taught Ephraim to walk, I took them in my arms; yet they have not understood that I was the one looking after them. I led them with reins of kindness, with leading-strings of love. I was like someone who lifts an infant close against his cheek; stooping down to him I gave him his food (Hos 11:1–4).

This depiction of God as mother to Israel is continued in several passages in Second Isaiah. Isaiah 49:15 compares God's care for Israel to a mother's care for her child.

> Does a woman forget her baby at the breast,
> or fail to cherish the son of her womb?
> Yet even if these forget,
> I will never forget you.

Just as God is portrayed as father in Deut 1:31 and 8:5, a rare usage in the Hebrew Scriptures, a passage in Isaiah 66:9–13, designates God as mother. God will bless Israel that they may "be suckled and filled, from her consoling breast," for God says, "Like a son comforted by his mother will I comfort you."

In her study *God and the Rhetoric of Sexuality* Phyllis Trible provides a thorough discussion of this motherly compassion and translates the poetry of Jeremiah 31:20 to reveal it more fully.

> Is Ephraim my dear Son? my darling child?
> For the more I speak of him,
>   the more do I remember him.
> Therefore, my womb trembles for him;

I will truly show motherly-compassion
upon him. Oracle of Yahweh.[12]

For the prophets, the full warmth and tenderness of God's care for Israel is best expressed in mother/father metaphors.

The Gospels, too, suggest such a portrayal of the character of God's care. In Luke's trio of parables depicting God's compassion for the lost, God is like the shepherd who goes in search of a single lost sheep, and like the father of the son who squanders his goods in a faraway land. God is also like the woman who searches for a lost coin (Lk 15:1–32). In another passage (Lk 13:34), Jesus makes the image of protecting wings a feminine image and applies it to himself: "Jerusalem, Jerusalem, you that kill the prophets and stone those who are sent to you! How often have I longed to gather your children, as a hen gathers her brood under her wings, and you refused!" These selections do not represent the major stream of images for God in the New Testament. However, they are part of Jesus' reversal of the attitudes toward women current in his time. They reinforce the fact that with Jesus' coming the kingdom of God has broken into history, transforming the old social order. In that kingdom male and female are both embraced and opened to new possibilities.

A fresh look at the biblical writings reveals other feminine imagery of God. Divine Wisdom is feminine grammatically in both Hebrew (*hokmah*) and Greek (*sophia*). In the wisdom literature, Wisdom is personified as a woman.

Wisdom calls aloud in the streets,
    she raises her voice in the public squares;
she calls out at the street corners,
    she delivers her message at the city gates.
"You ignorant people, how much longer
    will you cling to your ignorance?

> How much longer will mockers revel in their mocking
> and fools hold knowledge contemptible?" (Prov 1:20 ff).

Proverbs, Job, Baruch and Ben Sirach sing the praises of Lady Wisdom, and in the Gospels of Matthew and Luke, Jesus speaks of this feminine divine Wisdom.

> And that is why the Wisdom of God said, "I will send
> them prophets and apostles" (Lk 11:49; cf. Mt 11:18–19).

Along with Wisdom, the divine *ruach* or spirit is also a feminine noun (Wis 1:4–7; 7:21–22).

This is not an exhaustive list of feminine images for God, but it is enough to show that the biblical literature uses both male and female metaphors for God, keeping us aware that God transcends sexuality and cannot be identified with either sex. This enables men and women to relate to God and one another in new ways. The final goal of keeping alive a polyphony of images of God, impersonal and personal, male and female, stern and gentle, is to open us more fully to all aspects of the healing presence of God in our world. It is also the ultimate symbolism undergirding mutual respect and cooperation between men and women. Insisting on certain biblical images to the exclusion of others impoverishes everyone.

The Idol and the Image

In reflecting on some of the biblical images of God, we mentioned that they not only enrich, but also qualify and limit one another. This interaction of meanings is the imagination's language of analogy. As traditionally developed, the doctrine of analogy was meant to provide a way of speaking of God which allows for both similarity and difference between God and the human. We cannot apply human terms to God literally. But if our language can say nothing of God, if, for example, divine love in no way resembles human love, then we end in agnosticism. As St. Thomas Aquinas used analogy it became a sensitive way of describing God which neither equated the divine with our human reality nor declared that God was totally unlike it. All our language about God contains both an *is* and an *is not:* God *is* and *is not* like a father, mother, ocean, fire, or spouse. The use of many metaphors for God, female as well as male, prevents the exclusive development of any single metaphor, the turning of an image into an idol. In the words of Paul Ricoeur, the God we seek "is their common goal, which escapes each of them."[13] God remains larger than the confines of all language.

Thus, we do not believe *in* the images themselves; we see *through* them. If we do not see through them, they can get in the way and restrict our vision. An image or metaphor is like a lens through which we catch a glimpse of God. Since God is always revealed in symbol, we do not see God directly, but indirectly, through created things. This is the meaning of Paul's words in 1 Corinthians 13:12 when he reminds us that we see God now in a mirror dimly; later we will see "face to face." Mirrors in St. Paul's time were made of polished metal; hence, they produced a dark image. But the indirect language of the imagination can also hold together paradoxes which we are unable completely to understand, for example, that God is both merciful and just, terrible and gentle, transcendent and immanent. Isaiah speaks of a God who is near and yet ineffable.

> Seek Yahweh while he is still to be found,
>   call to him while he is still near.
> Let the wicked man abandon his way,
>   the evil man his thoughts.
> Let him turn back to Yahweh who will take pity on him,
>   to our God who is rich in forgiving;

> for my thoughts are not your thoughts,
>   my ways not your ways—it is Yahweh who speaks.
> Yes, the heavens are as high above the earth
>   as my ways are above your ways,
>   my thoughts above your thoughts (Is 55:6–9).

The theological notions of God's transcendence and immanence are here powerfully held together in one poetic passage.

Because God is eminently real but beyond definition or description, we will continue to search for new metaphors in our struggle to understand. One contemporary seeker is the Pulitzer Prize winning poet, Anne Sexton. She presents a dramatic example of the search that is part of the lives of many others. In her poem, "Not So. Not So," she writes: "I cannot walk an inch without trying to walk to God."[14] Anne Sexton desired a relationship with the Father, Son and Holy Spirit of the Christian tradition, but her poems show that she saw her personal predicament as an "exile from God." In "Rowing" she says,

> but I grew, I grew,
> and God was there like an island I had not rowed to.

And in "The Poet of Ignorance":

> Perhaps God is only a deep voice
> heard by the deaf,
> I do not know.[15]

In her quest Anne Sexton explored numerous images of God—The Island, Dearest Dealer, Laughter of the Morning—and seemed on the verge of seeing that no one name could contain God. The God-images found in her poetry, many of them challenging and unorthodox, are a reminder that tradition is not an unchanging legacy from the past, but a resource to be adapted to new circumstances and problems. Images can become idols not only when they are interpreted literally, but also when they cease to speak to a changing culture. To prevent this, a community needs to create metaphors which make available the power of the tradition in new ways. In our last section we will look at one contemporary attempt to do this—process theology.

God as Poet: Images of God in Process Theology

Like J.B. Phillips, process theologians believe that our God is too small. We have reduced the size of the divine by describing God in terms of only certain dimensions of experience, those that are controlling, active, independent. God acts on the world but receives nothing from it, and is wholly self-sufficient. Hence, process theology has its own list of inadequate names for God: Unchanging and Passionless, Controlling Power, Status Quo, Male.[16] Charles Hartshorne has argued that to say God is more perfect the more completely the divine is removed from change, risk, and time preserves a prejudice which contradicts our experience of divine love.[17] Love involves mutual interaction, the sharing of suffering and joy, creative activity in relation to another. The biblical God is one who loves and suffers with a people, and who continually attempts to persuade them to turn from evil and place their trust in that love. To qualify and enlarge inadequate descriptions of the divine, process theologians propose other analogies between human and divine experience, recognizing that they share the limitations of all such language. Their source is the images of God found in the writings of Alfred North Whitehead.

Whitehead felt that David Hume, in his *Dialogues Concerning Natural Religion*, had criticized unanswerably the three strains of thinking on God which Whitehead associates respectively with the divine Caesars, the Hebrew prophets, and Aristotle. God is not an imperial ruler, the personification of moral energy, or the ultimate philosophical principle. Whitehead finds in the Galilean origins of Christianity another suggestion for dealing with the question of God. It does not fit well, he believes, with the other three, for "it does not emphasize the ruling Caesar, or the ruthless moralist, or the unmoved mover. It dwells upon the tender elements in the world, which slowly and in quietness operate by love; and it finds purpose in the present immediacy of a kingdom not of this world."[18] Whitehead considered the essence of Christianity to be its appeal to Christ's life as revelation of the nature of God and the divine activity in the world. He believed that the tenderness, sympathy, and love revealed in Jesus' death disclosed the nature of that Divine Reality: God's activity is persuasive, not coercive, power. Whitehead intends to attribute to God the qualities which he finds exemplified in the Gospel accounts of Jesus.

In keeping with this intention, Whitehead speaks of God as "the poet of the world, with tender patience leading it by his vision of truth, beauty, and goodness."[19] This depiction of God as the Divine Poet is supplemented in Whitehead by images of God as the final wisdom, the final beauty of the universe and "the great companion—the fellow-sufferer who understands."[20] What does this cluster of images suggest? God as Poet is one whose love operates by persuasion, not by coercion. This love is the lure of ideals and values which others are moved to actualize. It is like the love of a parent. The prophet Hosea portrays it as leading "with reins of kindness, with leading-strings of love" (11:3). The power of such love lies in its capacity to evoke a response while respecting the integrity and freedom of others. God as Poet takes seriously the responsibility and adventure of time.

As Fellow Sufferer and Great Companion, God is a God

of real compassion. We have always believed that God cares for the world. However, process theology displaces the classical position that God affects the world but the world does not affect God. In process thought, there is both giving and receiving. God hears and responds, shares and suffers with creation. The psalmist captures this aspect of God's love.

> I waited and waited for Yahweh,
>   now at last he has stooped to me
>   and heard my cry for help (Ps 40:1).

God's essential nature does not change and the divine purpose is unchanging; nevertheless, events in the world really make a difference to God. God is one who suffers with us, who identifies with the oppressed. Unlike us, however, God knows the limits of all tragedy and the infinite resources available for dealing with evil.

Whitehead's references to God as the Final Wisdom and Final Beauty of the Universe are like the Book of Proverbs' admonitions to hold fast to Lady Wisdom.

> Acquire Wisdom, acquire Perception,
>   never forget her, never deviate from my words.
> Do not desert her, she will keep you safe,
>   love her, she will watch over you (Prov 4:5).

Like this biblical reference to Wisdom, Whitehead emphasizes the importance of a sustaining relationship with God as Final Wisdom and Final Beauty. God is the source both of the values which move individuals and civilizations, and of their movement toward these values. Whitehead's image of God as Final Wisdom means God's tender care and infinite patience that nothing be lost which can be saved. All that is done in the world is received by God, transformed in the divine love and unity, and offered again to the world.

A relationship to God as the Final Beauty of the Universe results in the experience of Peace. Such Peace is, according to Whitehead, a transcending of one's personality, a movement toward wider sympathies and the enlarging of one's love, and a calming of that turbulence which is destructive and inhibiting. Peace is not an escape from life's risks, but rather brings the will and power to meet them. In the midst of an existence filled with frustration, pain, and loss, Peace is the inner feeling which accompanies a grasp of the purpose of tragedy: "Amid the passing of so much beauty, so much heroism, so much daring, Peace is then the intuition of permanence."[21] The experience of God as Final Beauty is, again, like the following of Lady Wisdom.

> Happy the person who discovers Wisdom,
>   the person who gains discernment:
> Gaining her is more rewarding than silver,
>   more profitable than gold.
> She is beyond the price of pearls,
>   nothing you could covet is her equal.
> In her right hand is length of days;
>   in her left hand, riches and honour.
> Her ways are delightful ways,
>   her paths all lead to contentment.
> She is a tree of life for those who hold her fast,
>   those who cling to her live happy lives (Prov 3:13–18).

Such, in another idiom, is the Peace which Whitehead describes.

Whitehead grounds his images of God as Poet, Great Companion, Fellow Sufferer, Final Wisdom and Final Beauty of the Universe in a view of the world which he has developed through imaginative generalization. He describes a cosmos built on mutuality and interdependence. In such a world everything is related to, is affected by, and influences everything else. There is no reality, not even God, for whom a completely detached, self-contained existence is possible. The usual hierarchies and dualities are replaced by a network of relationships between interdependent beings. The central fact of all of existence is the individual in community. Whitehead's divine images support a life in which both activity and receptivity are valued as modes of love. The power to act is a part of love, but love also includes the ability to be acted upon and moved by another. We have not really loved unless we have been transformed in some way by our relationship to another.

We have seen how images of God shape the personal life and vision of believers. In an inclusive world such as Whitehead envisions, male and female do not designate superior and inferior spheres of experience. Mutuality is grounded in the divine life, in our relationship to the Poet of the world. Process theology's images of God do not say everything that can be said of God. As we have seen, no one image can do that. But they do enliven our common effort to speak to and about God in ways that free the human spirit.

By opening our imaginations anew in each age, we are able to reappropriate the traditional images of God in light of our contemporary context. As we listen anew we hear sounds of God's presence we have not heard before, melodies through which we sense something of the mystery of the divine. This polyphony of images lets God be God and calls humans to become all that they can be.

Notes

1. (New York: Macmillan Company, 1955).

2. (Philadelphia: Fortress Press, 1979), p. 104.

3. John Henry Newman, *Grammar of Assent* (New York: Doubleday & Company, 1955), p. 106.

4. See *Metaphor and Reality* (Bloomington: Indiana U. Press, 1962).

5. "Oratio Ad Sanctum Paulum." In *Patrologia Latina,* ed. J.P. Migne, Vol. 158, cols. 981ff.

6. Julian of Norwich, *Showings,* trans. Edmund Colledge, O.S.A. and James Walsh, S.J. (New York: Paulist Press, 1978), Chapter 58, p. 294. See also Eleanor McLaughlin, "Women, Power and the Pursuit of Holiness in Medieval Christianity," in *Women of Spirit,* ed. Rosemary Ruether and Eleanor McLaughlin (New York: Simon & Schuster, 1979), pp. 99–130.

7. "Should Women Be Ordained? No," *The Episcopalian* 137/2 (February 1972), 8.

8. Dietrich Bonhoeffer, *Letters and Papers From Prison,* ed. Eberhard Bethge (New York: The Macmillan Company, 1972), p. 311.

9. "Naming God," *Union Seminary Quarterly Review* 34/4 (Summer 1979), 222.

10. See Evelyn Underhill, *Mysticism* (5th ed., London: Methuen & Co., 1914) for the variety of such images.

11. A very complete and helpful summary of this imagery can be found in Leonard Swidler, *Biblical Affirmations of Woman* (Philadelphia: The Westminster Press, 1979).

12. (Philadelphia: Fortress Press, 1978), p. 45.

13. "Naming God," 222.

14. *The Awful Rowing Toward God* (Boston: Houghton Mifflin Company, 1975), p. 83.

15. *The Awful Rowing,* pp. 1, 28.

16. See John B. Cobb, Jr. and David Ray Griffin, *Process Theology: An Introductory Exposition* (Philadelphia: Westminster Press, 1976).

17. *Man's Vision of God* (New York: Harper & Brothers, 1941).

18. Alfred North Whitehead, *Process and Reality* (New York: The Macmillan Company, 1969), p. 404.

19. *Process and Reality,* p. 408.

20. *Adventures of Ideas* (New York: The Macmillan Company, 1967), pp. 284–296; *Process and Reality,* pp. 410, 413.

21. *Adventures of Ideas,* p. 286.

VII. Imagination and Morality

What forces move human beings to action? We find this an especially pressing question today in face of the erosion of values, escalation of violence, and prospect of nuclear disaster which mark our age. For Christians, questions regarding the wellsprings of human behavior have an added urgency: How can we shape our choices according to the mind of Christ? How do we effectively insert Gospel values into our present arena of competing value systems?

Concerned with issues such as these, Christian educators and parents of the 1960's and 1970's turned for help to writings on value clarification and moral development. Works such as *Values and Teaching*, published in 1966 by Louis Raths, Merrill Harmin, and Sidney Simon, promised assistance in the task of transmitting values. However, value-clarifying techniques delivered only part of their promise. They did provide a process whereby individuals could come to see more clearly the values they actually espouse, and so possess these values more consciously and act on them more consistently. But participants in the process of value clarification discovered that understanding one's present values is not enough. If we are to mold our life according to the Gospel, we need a vision which enables us to change.

Lawrence Kohlberg's theory of moral development provided another popular approach to moral education. Central to Kohlberg's theory is the conviction that the ability to make mature moral judgments requires the capacity for sophisticated moral reasoning. The predominant method of learning he suggests is the rational analysis of moral dilemmas. Faced with a moral dilemma, what will you choose to do and why? The reasons given for an action, such as fear of punishment, desire to please others, concern for a contract, or commitment to universal justice, are the distinguishing marks of the different stages of moral development. A helpful tool in many ways, Kohlberg's method nevertheless fails to engage fully the deeper levels of a person's moral motivation. Two of Kohlberg's closest collaborators, Donald Oliver and Mary Jo Bane, are among those critical of his emphasis on the rational, linear, and discursive treatment of moral dilemmas. They know that moral reasoning is not the equivalent of moral sensitivity. In their article "Moral Education—Is Reasoning Enough?" Oliver and Bane emphasize the indispensability of non-rational and non-discursive elements in moral development.[1]

The limitations of these approaches to moral education, as well as experience of our own moral life, provide evidence that the springs of human action are deeper, more difficult to change, and less susceptible to argument than is usually acknowledged. We are beginning to recognize that the deepest sources of our moral behavior are found in the life of the imagination. Human deeds begin in the imagination; it is there that our lives are shaped. Consequently, as Paul Ricoeur has said, "any ethic that addresses the will in order to demand a decision must be subject to a poetry that opens up new dimensions for the imagination."[2] Principles and rules are necessary in our moral life. However, we live most deeply from our images, rituals, and stories, and these are more difficult to change than our laws and principles.

In this chapter we will examine some of the ways in

which the life of the imagination is crucial to our ethical venture. In showing how imagination is linked to our moral life, the chapter explores three themes: (1) Imagination and Hope: What Things Seem Possible? (2) Imagination and Character: Whom Do I Want To Be Like? (3) Imagination and Justice: What Does It Feel Like To Be the Other?

Imagination and Hope: What Things Seem Possible?

Future survival depends on our capacity to rehearse alternate possibilities for existence. A civilization that is locked into established patterns of energy consumption, and violence as a solution to conflict, can continue to hope only if it sees alternate worlds to our present one. It is the imagination which opens up such possibilities for our personal and communal actions. Nothing is possible until we have first imagined it. Again, the Bible embodies the necessary approach. Many of the biblical writings highlight this link between imagination, possibility, and moral action. Some examples from the prophets, Jesus, and Paul will illustrate how it is a key characteristic of their appeals for moral conversion.

The kingdoms of Israel and Judah, from the ninth to the sixth century B.C., were caught in the pincers of internal corruption and external oppression. Both king and commoner had betrayed Israel's highest ideals. How could this people rise from its spiritual and moral ruins to live again? The task of calling Israel and Judah to a deep conversion of heart fell to prophets like Amos, Isaiah, Jeremiah and Micah. The language they speak is largely the language of poetry. They appeal to the imagination of a people.

The biblical scholar Walter Brueggemann illustrates this prophetic practice of imagination with reference to the text of Micah 4:1–5.

> They will hammer their swords into ploughshares,
>   their spears into sickles.
> Nation will not lift sword against nation;
>   there will be no more training for war.
> Each man will sit under his vine and his fig tree,
>   with no one to trouble him.

Micah makes a prophetic promise which is meant to lead Israel to an alternative reality. Brueggemann believes that the employment of such imagination by the prophet does two things: it invites Israel to contemplate inexplicable futures, beyond human engineering, which God may yet give, and it reminds Israel that the present system is not the last word, not absolute. We urgently need such prophetic imagination today to challenge two of the same conditions Micah addresses: the use of war as a solution for international conflicts, and a social order which allows the rich to trample on the rights of the poor. The dreams and hopes conveyed by the poet Micah are for a disarmed world, an end to the public policy of war, and a dismantling of the war apparatus. Along with this hope goes the hope for a transformed human consciousness and personal agrarian well-being "under vine and fig tree." The word of the prophet creates a sphere of freedom for the imagination of Israel, allowing her to see how life may yet be ordered.[3] The prophetic imagination is the basis for Israel's hope, providing her with radical alternatives for the future and challenging present social policy in light of those alternatives.

The prophets issue a moral challenge to Israel by another use of the imagination: reference to the stories which were the ancient basis of the Torah, stories which also frame our own moral decisions. In raising their central moral question—How does God act and how should the people act?—prophets such as Amos, Hosea, Micah, Jeremiah, Isaiah, and Ezekiel recall the story of God's mighty actions in calling Israel's fathers, freeing the Israelite slaves from Egypt, guiding them in the desert, and leading them into the land provided for them.

> It was I who brought you out of the land of Egypt and for forty years led you through the wilderness to take possession of the Amorites' country (Am 2:10).

This larger story provides the frame of reference for answering the question, "What are we to do?" It is moral exhortation in the form of a story.

Along with these stories and poetic promises, there are other examples of the way in which Israel's prophets, in their efforts to goad Israel's conscience, appeal to the imagination. They employ striking images and metaphors: the self-indulgent and securely rich "lying on ivory beds and sprawling on their divans" (Am 6:4), sins that are scarlet becoming white as snow (Is 1:18). They carry out symbolic actions to dramatize their prophecy: Ezekiel scratches a city on a brick and uses it to act out the siege of Jerusalem (4:1ff); Jeremiah smashes an earthen pot to signify the coming destruction of Judah (19:1–15) and buys some land to express his confidence in Judah's future even as things look their bleakest (32:6ff); Isaiah goes about naked and barefoot, in the condition of a deportee, to warn of Judah's impending captivity (20:1ff); Hosea's marriage to a faithless wife symbolizes Israel's own infidelity. By such imaginative speech and action Israel's prophets tie their ethical injunctions to concrete possibilities and provide alternative visions to shape the future. Contemporary prophets use symbolic actions too to awaken our moral sensitivities: pouring blood on draft files to dramatize opposition to war; wearing masks of death in marches which protest American military involvement in third world nations; hammering on instruments of war to move us to disarm; establishing symbols of peace, such as Ground Zero, as centers of non-violent resistance to nuclear buildup. In trying to bring moral change, these prophets appeal primarily to the imagination. Like Martin Luther King, they "have a dream" of what the future could be.

In issuing his challenge to live according to the new standards of the kingdom, Jesus also engages the imaginations of his listeners. The metaphor of the kingdom itself invites his hearers to envision a different future, one in which bonds of love, justice, and peace prevail. Like the prophets before him, Jesus creates hope by showing a different vision.

He also expresses his ethical command in the shape of story. In describing this link between moral challenge and story in the New Testament, Amos Wilder notes how

> these stories span our lives and wait our answer. To use a slang expression, they "put us on the spot." The stories are so graphic that we are bound hand and foot. Our consciences must stand and deliver. What is interesting here is the suggestion that it takes a good story to make people realize what the right thing to do is. The road to a moral judgment is by way of the imagination![4]

As we saw in the chapter on prayer and imagination, Jesus' most original story form is the parable. In answering a question or responding to a concern about the kingdom, Jesus tells a parable. The parables draw us into the particular details of an ordinary human situation in such a way that they allow us to transcend that situation. As John Dominic Crossan has pointed out, they subvert our world and call in question our usual way of seeing things.[5] In hearing the story of the laborers in the vineyard (Mt 20:1–16), in which those who have not arrived on the scene until the third, sixth, and ninth hours are offered the same pay as those hired early in the morning, we are forced to ask: Does God play by our rules? The extravagant actions of the father of the prodigal son (Lk 15:11–32), who runs out to meet a wayward boy, calls a feast, and heaps gifts upon a runaway, challenges us to reconsider the way we act when we are wronged. The parables force us to participate in moral dilemmas whose solutions will contain unsettling surprises and overturn our expectations.

The range of motivation and behavior found in Jesus' parables is such that we all recognize ourselves in the characters and their dilemmas. But the parables do not deal primarily with major crises in life. Nor is that the sphere where most of our moral decisions and actions take place. Crossan has suggested that their approach be seen as fundamental morality.[6] Such a morality is concerned with the moral *dimensions* of the world around us: relationships between fathers and sons, or landlords and tenants; the problems of widows on fixed incomes; the struggle to show compassion when it means taking personal risks. These are stories of everyday life lived in the presence of God, not lists of dos and don'ts. They show us what that presence means across a wide spectrum of situations in which we live with others and interact with them. They allow us to ponder our motives and actions within a context where God's perspective is part of the texture of the story itself. It is this perspective which opens up new possibilities for our imagination, shapes our moral vision, and sustains our hope.

Paul's first letter to the Christians at Corinth provides another example of the way in which imaginative language can motivate people, calling forth new attitudes and actions. In this letter Paul uses the metaphor of the body of Christ to deal with a wide variety of problems in the Corinthian community.[7] He borrows the stoic metaphor of the whole cosmos as a body and applies it to the Christian community.

You know, surely, that your bodies are members making up the body of Christ (1 Cor 6:16).

This body imagery enables the Corinthians to understand their personal, social, and liturgical experience in a new way. That is exactly what Paul is striving to accomplish: to bring about a reorientation of the Christian life in Corinth. The question of how Christians should view their bodily existence lies behind many of the ethical problems of the Corinthians. The prevailing Hellenistic view divided the human being into an immortal spirit or mind, a mortal soul, and a material body that imprisoned the mind and kept it from its true divinity. Paul wants to show that indifference to the material body is not a mark of the spiritual person. He presents the image of the body as a temple of the Holy Spirit, not to be abused in sexual offenses such as incest and prostitution (1 Cor 6:1–20). The Christian Eucharist is participation in the body of Christ; it excludes participation in the banquets honoring pagan deities and is incompatible with failure to share food with the hungry (1 Cor 8; 11:17–36). The Church is the body of Christ; the variety of personal gifts given to the community are for the sake of building up this body (1 Cor 12). Finally, Christians await a bodily resurrection. The body metaphor culminates in the resurrected body of the new creation (1 Cor 15), which signifies that everything we know now will be preserved and transformed rather than simply cast off and replaced. By appealing to their imagination in this way, Paul has provided the Corinthians with an organizing vision which will link the parts of their lives into a whole, a vision which will enable them to move beyond their present ethical limitations. Metaphor is Paul's mode of suggesting new possibilities.

The imaginative vision of the prophets, Jesus, and Paul continues to present us with alternate possibilities for our own existence. In addition, their use of the language of the imagination provides a pattern for our contemporary moral efforts. It challenges us to use all of the imaginative resources of our own age in sustaining hope. Both in content, and in style or rhetoric, they show us how we might answer the question, "What things are possible?"

This first section has concentrated primarily on the relationship between imagination and possibility. Imagination is also characterized by its connection with wholeness and patterns of value, rather than the immediacy of particular actions. It is imagination which enables us to link our individual deeds with what we might be or not be as a self. We will look next at the implications of this aspect of the imagination in terms of its influence in character formation.

Imagination and Character: Whom Do I Want To Be Like?

We use the term "character" in a number of different ways. Sometimes we say that a person "has character," or that she "showed her true character" in an action. Or we believe that certain actions "develop character." The unifying element in our many uses of the word is a conviction that an ongoing personal identity underlies one's particular actions. We expect certain friends to deal honestly with us because they are trustworthy. We mistrust even the good actions of others because they seem out of character with what they have revealed of themselves in other ways. In discussing the relationship between imagination and character in this section, we will use the term "character" to refer to our moral identity or personal being. Particular actions both flow from and shape this identity. Character includes more than our actions; it describes our inner motives and intentions as well. Our character is the person we are becoming.[8]

Until recently, discussions of morality have concentrated chiefly on the analysis of principles and rules and the particular choices based on these. For example, we were concerned with the concrete application of such principles as: we can only be morally responsible when we have knowledge and freedom, or, the end does not justify the means. We also sought careful definitions of our moral terms—right and wrong, good and evil, sin and virtue, mortal and venial—and looked for answers to questions such as what makes an action right or wrong and what place law holds in a Christian ethic. The formation of character received much less attention than these matters of the mind. Now this emphasis is changing. We are attentive again to the fact that a person's morality is not simply a matter of rules and principles. Each of us acts from a total moral vision. We act the way we do because of our vision of the world. Change in human behavior requires a transformation of that vision. The novelist Iris Murdoch, in her many reflections on the relationship between vision and choice in morality, emphasizes that this total vision of life is something elusive. We recognize its presence in other people "as shown in their mode of speech or silence, their choice of words, their assessments of others, their conception of their own lives, what they think attractive or praiseworthy, what they think funny: in short, the configurations of their thought which show continually in their reactions and conversation."9 The notion of vision is one way of describing the pattern of our personal becoming. From this viewpoint, the moral life is a way of seeing the world, and differences in morality result from different perspectives.

Another dimension of our moral identity is our orientation or direction in life. We gradually deepen our basic choice to love or to withdraw in selfishness. Whereas the notion of vision emphasizes seeing, this idea of a fundamental option puts more stress on choosing. Our fundamental option is the free determination we make of ourselves with respect to the whole of existence. Bernard Haring, in *Free and Faithful in Christ*, describes it as an ethics of the heart.

God does not want only external deeds. True morality arises from basic freedom, that fundamental commitment of self that becomes a transcendental freedom giving ultimate meaning and direction to one's free choice in the concrete situation.... A good decision and the right deed express morality in the full sense only when the act comes from one's heart where the fundamental option is for God and good, and reaches into that depth where one turns in the right direction.[10]

This heart of the person is an inner center of energy, and its quality is determined by the values we internalize on that deepest level. An ethics of the heart views the moral life not as a series of disconnected actions or omissions, but as a process of personal orientation.

Whether we look at our identity in terms of our vision or of our fundamental option, we are dealing with the moral life in its wholeness. Standing behind and before our individual choices and actions is a total perspective on life and a total direction for life, what T. S. Eliot in "East Coker" refers to as

... Not the intense moment
Isolated, with no before and after,
But a lifetime burning in every moment....[11]

But how do we influence this level of moral wholeness? It is here that the importance of the imagination for morality is once again clear. For imaginative forms touch us on just such deeper levels of personal becoming. Reflection on the power of two modes of the imagination will show us how this is so: Both ritual and literature shape our character in essential ways.

The connection between ritual and morality is an ancient one. Ritual is the public enactment by which a society communicates its values on the deepest and most critical level. In so doing, it answers for each new generation the question: What kind of person am I to be? We are familiar with the rites of initiation which are obligatory for members of a society. The story of Black Elk, a Sioux Indian shaman who lived in the last of the nineteenth and beginning of the twentieth centuries, describes an initiatory illness through which he hears his call to be a spiritual leader and healer of his people. For days he lies in a coma, receiving the vision. Then he must find a way to share the powerful experience with his people.[12] The film *Walkabout* depicts the custom among Australian aborigines of sending the teenage boy alone into the wild for one hundred days to survive by his wits. When he returns, he is no longer a boy in his society but a man. The function of such rites of passage is to effect the transition from childhood or adolescence to adulthood. Mircea Eliade points out how in archaic societies it is through initiation rites that a person becomes what he or she is and should be. Through initiation a child is introduced to spiritual values, to the whole body of the tribe's cultural and mythological traditions: "It is a fundamental existential experience because through it a man becomes able to assume his mode of being in its entirety."[13] The initiation ritual is not for the young only; it involves the tribe as a whole. The repetition of the traditional rites regenerates the entire community. That is why initiations are such important religious festivals.

This same capacity of ritual to mold vision and identity is apparent in Israel's covenant ceremonies. When Moses ratifies the Sinai covenant, he directs the people to offer communion sacrifices to the Lord. He then pours half of the blood of the sacrifice on the altar and sprinkles the other half on the people, impressing upon them how they have bonded themselves with God. The people accept the covenant obligations and assume a new identity in terms of it. Later liturgies of

covenant renewal confront the community with the necessity
of a radical interiorization of the whole covenant tradition.

> The Word is very near to you, it is in your mouth and in
> your heart for your observance.... Choose life, then, so
> that you and your descendants may live, in the love of
> Yahweh your God, obeying his voice, clinging to him ...
> (Dt 30:14, 19).

Such covenant renewals illustrate how ritual enables us to
draw on our own memories and those around us to find that
continuity on which we depend for a sense of identity.

The Christian liturgy is the ritual central to our life of
faith. It is a form of remembering which touches us in our total
context: body and spirit, individual and social. As a celebration
of the life, death, and resurrection of Jesus, it throws the light
of the Gospel on our moral dilemmas. We are reminded of the
deeper meaning of discipleship and at the same time shaped
according to its demands. This is Christian character formation.

Central to the way in which liturgy forms our identity is
the fact that in it we rehearse the great narratives of our faith.
Liturgy is the setting for telling the stories which provide our
life vision. We root ourselves in the experiences of Israel's
journey with God. We retell stories from Jesus' life, the details
of his passion, death, and resurrection, and accounts of disciples who followed him. In his article on "Liturgy and Ethics,"
Paul Ramsey illustrates this point by relating the Christian
liturgy to the problem of abortion.

> Far more than any argument, it was surely the power of
> the Nativity Stories and their place in ritual and celebra-
> tion and song that tempered the conscience of the West to
> its audacious effort to wipe out the practice of abortion

and infanticide.... From the correct version heard and
sung and dramatized, generations of men and women
learned to feel and think of their own unborn children in a
very special way. The Nativity Narratives served as a
model for human beginnings, just as the creation of a
people out of Egypt did for Genesis, Jeremiah, and the
Psalms.[14]

Liturgy, Ramsey believes, not only transforms our perspectives and character in a general way; it also presents us with
substantial moral content.

This description of the potential of ritual to influence
morality may seem ideal. Liturgy could do this, but in fact it
does not. The loss of the power of ritual in our lives is in itself
a symptom of the loss of imagination. When symbol and story
no longer have power in our lives, it is difficult to appreciate
the importance of ritual. Ritual is not an activity which
achieves visible results; it therefore loses significance in a
society bent on productivity. In discussing the relationship of
the arts to spirituality, we stressed that artists are essential if
we are to retain a sacramental vision. They also keep alive the
sensitivities that enable us to enter into ritual.

However, part of the answer lies with our liturgy itself.
The imagination and its forms of language can live only in the
midst of concrete particulars. If liturgy becomes too universal
and standardized it loses its power to convey basic values in a
specific cultural setting. For internalization of values to take
place within a multi-cultural Christianity, more diversity in
the specifics of ritual celebration must be allowed. Walter
Buhlmann refers to this issue in *The Coming of the Third
Church* when he pleads for pluriformity in unity in the
Church. For example, the use of native music, symbols, and
languages in the liturgies of African, Asian, and Latin American churches will not destroy basic unity in faith: "On the

contrary, it consists in implanting Christ's message in that cultural environment, in a new creation springing from that way of life, an *incarnation* within an existing way of life."[15] The use of alien forms destroys the imaginative power of liturgical symbols.

Ritual, then, is one way in which the imagination can mold our moral identity. A second imaginative expression which shapes our character is literature in its many forms: fairy tales, novels, short stories, dramas. G. K. Chesterton writes in *Orthodoxy* that he learned his first and most lasting philosophy in the nursery, through fairy tales. He finds a morality inherent in fairy tales—for example, the great lesson of "Beauty and the Beast," that "a thing must be loved *before* it is lovable."[16] In his study of *The Uses of Enchantment,* Bruno Bettelheim suggests several ways in which fairy tales contribute to a child's moral development. Of prime importance is the fact that they relate to all aspects of the child's personality. Facing life's challenges requires that all of our inner resources, our emotions, imagination, and intellect, support and enrich one another. Fairy tales provide images for our inner experiences; they allow us to feel anxious when a hero or heroine is challenged by a dreadful danger, and to suffer as they face an unbearable fate without hope of happiness. Fairy tales are symbolic expressions of important life experiences.

In addition, fairy tales provide heroes and heroines with which a child can identify. The reader of the fairy tale answers the question "Whom do I want to be like?" by projecting herself wholeheartedly into a character such as Snow White or Cinderella. Although evil may appear to win out temporarily in a tale, as with the wicked stepmother in "Cinderella," or the jealous queen in "Snow White and the Seven Dwarfs," these evil forces are finally defeated. But the moral impact of the tale comes not so much from the fact that virtue triumphs and evil is punished in the end, but in the child's identification with the inner and outer struggles of the heroine. Fairy tales also enable us to confront the basic human predicaments such as limits, aging, and death; they show "that a struggle against severe difficulties in life is unavoidable, is an intrinsic part of human existence—but that if one does not shy away, but steadfastly meets unexpected and often unjust hardships, one masters all obstacles and in the end emerges victorious."[17] The story of "Puss'n Boots" recounts how the youngest of three sons inherits only a seemingly worthless tomcat; his brothers get all the worldly riches. They ridicule him, but he gives in to the cat's wishes and buys him a pair of boots with his last pennies. With these boots the cat can travel miles in seconds. The son who lacked all material security discovers a new and wider world, and eventually gains the hand of the king's daughter as well as the kingdom. In a similar tale, "The Three Feathers," by the Brothers Grimm, a king who has become old and weak is thinking of his end. Not knowing which of his three sons should inherit the kingdom after him, he decides to give each of them a difficult task. The one who succeeds best will become the next king. The two older brothers are afraid of the risk, and so never gain the kingdom, which goes to the youngest brother.

This power of fairy tales to affect the development of character in the child results, Bettelheim believes, from their literary qualities, their nature as works of art. C. S. Lewis would add that the power of such literary forms for all ages lies partly in their indirectness. This enables them to slip past our barriers and prejudices against more direct expressions of moral and religious truth. We experience the power of self-sacrificial love in Lewis' *The Lion, the Witch, and the Wardrobe*, even when we are closed to hearing the Gospel story.

All great literature shares the fairy tale's capacity to shape identity by lodging in the deep recesses of the self where our behavior is determined. It does this partly through its characters. A character is, in Wesley Kort's phrase, "an image of human possibilities, a paradigm of what man is, can be, should be, or must be."[18] Literary characters show us our human potential for good and evil. In Shakespeare's *Hamlet* we struggle with the relationship between appearance and reality, the difficulty of distinguishing between the appearance of wisdom, virtue, or right action, and their actuality. From Hamlet's opening "I know not 'seems'," we are drawn into his hatred of hypocrisy and deception, his effort to distinguish between genuine heroism and its showy counterfeits, and his struggle to bring about justice without being poisoned by hatred and vengefulness. In a similar way, we are disturbed, moved, and altered by Anna Karenina's struggle to deal with the consequences of choosing to go with Vronsky in Tolstoy's novel.

> Standing still, and looking at the tops of the aspen trees waving in the wind, with their freshly washed, brightly shining leaves in the cold sunshine, she knew that they would not forgive her, that everyone and everything would be merciless to her now as was that sky, that green. And again she felt that everything was split in two in her soul.[19]

We participate in the events leading to Anna's suicide, but without being involved in the consequences such events carry with them in the actual world. Through such characters we enter imaginatively into the conflict and drama of human existence; we experience the causes and signs of moral triumph and disaster.

This power of works of literature to influence our moral vision is especially evident in the case of autobiography, through lives like those of Ignatius Loyola, Dietrich Bonhoeffer, Thérèse of Lisieux, Helen Keller, Black Elk, or Maya Angelou. In *Design and Truth in Autobiography,* Roy Pascal speaks of aesthetic or artistic truth as the truth not of knowing but of being, since it has to do not primarily with knowing something, but with living life.[20] It is the power of such lived truth which accounts for the importance of autobiography in our character formation.

Autobiography is also one of the chief ways in which the community transmits its values to us. James McClendon emphasizes this point in developing an ethics of character in his book *Biography as Theology.*

> In or near the community there appear from time to time singular or striking lives, the lives of persons who embody the convictions of the community, but in a new way; who share the vision of the community, but with a new scope or power; who exhibit the style of the community, but with significant differences.[21]

Through contact with such lives individuals enlarge their moral vision and discover what such theological notions as redemption and grace mean when they are embedded in the concrete particulars of lived experience. Such lives provide not only a sense of possibility but also a realization of the ambiguity and complexity of moral decisions.

We began this section by looking at the importance of character or personal identity in our moral life. The question "Whom do I want to be like?" is a question whose answer molds our total vision and orientation in the moral life. It shapes our personal becoming. Answers to this question occur most deeply at the level of images, and we have seen how two imaginative forms, ritual and literature, influence these answers. Both reach the whole person. Ritual is a source of continuity and a setting for rehearsing the formative narratives of faith. Literature enables us to identify with characters who carry out moral decisions in the ambiguity and mystery of concrete lives. One aspect of ritual and literature which we

have not treated in this section is their impact on our affec-
tions and emotions. In the last part of this chapter we will deal
with the importance of the imagination for feeling and emotion with reference to a central area of the moral life, the
concern for justice.

Imagination and Justice:
What Does It Feel Like To Be the Other?

One reason we do not know how to choose is that we do
not know how to feel. Conscience is not simply an intellectual
event, but a judgment which involves the whole person. Both
our first awareness of a moral choice and our growing commitment to it have emotional roots. In addition, emotional energy
is vital as a support for decision and commitment.

Artistic expression has power to educate this inner order
of sensibility and feeling in a unique way. Nathan Scott says it
well in speaking of the literary artist, who

> asks us to look, indeed to stare, at *this* boy in love, at *this*
> plane soaring through the sky, at *this* soldier's fright be-
> fore the advance to the front—and he asks us to contem-
> plate these images so steadily and with such intentness
> that we begin to perceive the story or the fragment of a
> story in which they are interacting. Which is to say that he
> compels us to perform an act of judgment, and this not at
> the top of our minds but at the deep level of feeling, of
> passion, of sensibility, where the men and women of our
> generation are perhaps most in need of reeducation.[22]

Works of the imagination are essential in developing our
ability to be moved, amused, angered, persuaded, and elated.
This education of our sensibilities is vital to all moral growth,
but especially to a life-style of justice.

Lawrence Kohlberg describes those persons who have

reached what he calls the sixth stage of moral development or the stage of moral maturity as having several personality attributes. Their prime characteristic is a strong capacity for empathy. Such empathy is the basis of justice. The same point is underscored in Frederick Herzog's writings on liberation theology: "Opening up new dimensions for the imagination is the foremost challenge of systematic theology as liberation theology in North America."[23] These new dimensions of the imagination must take into account the non-person, those who struggle to become free subjects and take part in the transformation of their society: the dispossessed of Latin America, blacks, women, Mexican Americans. What both authors illustrate is that the ethical commandment of justice cannot be fulfilled without the imagination. Christian love of any kind requires the capacity to enter imaginatively into the life of others. It is the way we share the plight of those who differ from us, whether they be the homosexual, the American Indian, the poor who struggle against hunger, or the elderly who can move only slowly and with difficulty.

The imagination is essential to justice on several levels. First of all, it allows us to enter into the life, feelings, needs, and hopes of other persons and consciously will their good. This is true even of those we dislike. John Dewey makes this point in *Art as Experience* by stating that a holistic appreciation of another person is attainable only if we grasp the other person through the imagination.[24] Or, as the literary critic Cleanth Brooks says:

> Literature always involves an *as-if.* The literary mode is par excellence that in which we learn what it feels like to be in a certain situation. Literature has always been, therefore, the prime instrument for understanding other men and other cultures and other value systems.[25]

The words of both authors are movingly confirmed in the depiction of the brutal atrocities of the holocaust found in Elie Wiesel's autobiographical narrative, *Night.*

> Never shall I forget that night, the first night in camp, which has turned my life into one long night, seven times cursed and seven times sealed. Never shall I forget that smoke. Never shall I forget the little faces of the children, whose bodies I saw turned into wreaths of smoke beneath a silent blue sky.[26]

The impact of the narrative is in terms of concrete scenes and feelings, a boy's despair and an exhaustion of meaning in the world unlike anything previously encountered.

The imagination sustains a life-style of justice, then, by allowing us to enter into the experiences of others. But it is crucial that this entry be in terms of individuals and not generalities. Artistic expression deals always with the individual and particular. It allows the individual to exist with autonomy and self-assertion.[27] Art is open to this child, this city, this woman, in all of their uniqueness; its tendency is therefore against stereotypes, clichés, and prejudice. The ability to imagine and value what is distinctively individual in another frees us from intolerance and indifference toward what is alien and other. Such a sensitizing prepares us to welcome the non-person of whom Herzog speaks. This non-person is no longer a universal abstraction, but Connie Ramos, the Mexican American woman in Marge Piercy's novel *Woman on the Edge of Time,* who, as one of the powerless in a world of the powerful, is held against her will in a mental hospital. The non-person is the man of the broken tribe, the native who has died leaving wife and child bereft, in Alan Paton's novel of South Africa, *Cry the Beloved Country.*

Art helps us to feel for moral and social issues, not in their abstract and general aspects, but in terms of their effects on particular human situations. This power is found in the works of the artist Ben Shahn. Shahn was committed to human well-being and justice for all. One of his prints is titled, "I Think Continually of Those Who Were Truly Great," and is a tribute to ten civil rights martyrs. A brown and white serigraph, it shows a large dove of peace suspended in flight. The names of the martyrs are written at the top in a child-like script. Shahn's art is an example of the way in which such universal values as love, justice, and peace can be movingly portrayed in particular people and events. Part of the imagination's power to refine our feelings stems from the relationship between the way in which we see something and our emotional response to it. The American Indian artist, Eanger Irving Couse, who died in 1936, shows us this. Through paintings such as "Peace Pipe" and "Elk Foot of the Taos Tribe," charged as they are with a loving faith in the American Indian, he spoke to the sensitivities of our time and helped to bring about a reversal of consciousness. He created an image of the Indian as beautiful and noble.

This last section has focused on one dimension of imaginative works, their emotional power, in relation to justice in the moral life. In doing so, it accents themes that have been a part of the first two sections of the chapter as well. For in looking at the relationship of imagination to human possibility, personal identity, and the education of sensibilities, we are really treating one theme. That is the importance of taking into account the whole person when considering moral action. When pondering the springs of human behavior we must look first to the images, parables, stories, and rituals which shape our moral responses at their deepest levels.

The challenge of our time is to bring the power of Christ's message to bear on the pressing moral issues we face.

The imagination is crucial to this task. For it is in terms of the imagination that we find answers to three key questions in our moral life: What things seem possible? Whom do I want to be like? What does it feel like to be the other?

Notes

1. In *Moral Education,* ed. C. M. Beck, B. S. Crittenden, and E. J. Sullivan (New York: Newman Press, 1971), esp. pp. 258–260.

2. Quoted by Frederick Herzog in "Liberation and Imagination," *Interpretation. A Journal of Bible and Theology* 32 (July 1978), 228.

3. Walter Brueggemann, " 'Vine and Fig Tree': A Case Study in Imagination and Criticism," *The Catholic Biblical Quarterly* 43 (April 1981), pp. 188–204.

4. *Early Christian Rhetoric* (Cambridge: Harvard U. Press, 1971), p. 60.

5. See *The Dark Interval. Towards a Theology of Story* (Illinois: Argus Communications, 1975).

6. *Finding Is the First Act: Trove Folktales and Jesus' Treasure Parable* (Philadelphia: Fortress Press, 1979), pp. 114–116.

7. See Pheme Perkins, "Metaphor and Community," *The American Ecclesiastical Review* 169 (April 1975), 270–281.

8. For reflections on the meaning of character see Stanley Hauerwas, "Toward an Ethics of Character," *Vision and Virtue: Essays in Christian Ethical Reflection* (Notre Dame: Fides Publishers, Inc., 1974), pp. 48–67.

9. "Vision and Choice in Morality." In *Christian Ethics and Contemporary Philosophy,* ed. Ian T. Ramsey (New York: Macmillan Co., 1966), p. 202.

10. Vol. I, *General Moral Theology* (New York: Seabury Press, 1978), p. 186.

11. *The Complete Poems and Plays: 1909–1950* (New York: Harcourt, Brace & World, Inc.), p. 129.

12. John G. Neihardt, *Black Elk Speaks* (Lincoln, Neb.: U. of Nebraska Press, 1961).

13. *Rites and Symbols of Initiation: The Mysteries of Birth and Rebirth,* trans. Willard R. Trask (New York: Harper & Row, Torchbooks, 1965), p. 3.

14. *Journal of Religious Ethics* 7 (1979), 162–163.

15. (New York: Orbis Books, 1977), p. 287.

16. (New York: Doubleday & Company, 1959), p. 50.

17. Bruno Bettelheim, *The Uses of Enchantment: The Meaning and Importance of Fairy Tales* (New York: Vintage Books, 1977), p. 8.

18. *Narrative Elements and Religious Meaning* (Philadelphia: Fortress Press, 1975), p. 56.

19. Leo Tolstoy, *Anna Karenina* (New York: Grosset and Dunlap, 1931), p. 392.

20. (Cambridge: Harvard U. Press, 1960), p. 181.

21. (New York: Abingdon Press, 1974), p. 37.

22. "Art and the Renewal of Human Sensibility in Mass Society." In *Christian Faith and the Contemporary Arts,* ed. Finley Eversole (New York: Abingdon Press, 1962), p. 26.

23. "Liberation and Imagination," p. 228.

24. (New York: Capricorn Books, 1958), p. 348.

25. "Christianity, Myth, and the Symbolism of Poetry." In *Christian Faith and the Contemporary Arts,* p. 105.

26. Trans. Stella Rodway (New York: Avon Books, 1969), p. 44.

27. See Arthur J. Newman, "Aesthetic Sensitizing and Moral Education," *Journal of Aesthetic Education* 14/2 (April 1980), pp. 93–101.

VIII. Imagination and Ministry

Christian ministry takes a variety of forms. As ministers, we preach, teach, counsel, and celebrate. As the shape of ministry continues to expand, we stand on the edge of kinds of ministry we cannot yet envision. In and through these changing forms of ministry one thing seems certain, however. Every minister must be a tender of the inner rainbow, one who nurtures the life of the imagination. We have seen how central imagination is for several areas of Christian life: Scripture, spirituality, prayer, morality, our image of self, and our images of God. Imagination is the key to a living faith. Consequently, no one who ignores it can minister effectively.

Being a tender of rainbows in a time when Christians are just discovering again the importance of the imagination presents a twofold challenge. First, we must love and trust our own powers of imagination and be at home in the world of metaphor, poetry, image, and art. Hence, programs in training for ministry will need courses which can unlock our imaginative resources. Once we have experienced the power of the imagination in our own life of faith, it is easier to meet the second challenge. That is to open others to the treasures that lie at the end of their own inner rainbows. We said earlier that much of Western civilization is still afraid of dragons. We mistrust the life of the imagination. It may therefore take courage for the minister to preach, teach, or counsel through story, image, or art. It will require patience and trust to lead others gently to discover the power that these forms can have in their life of faith. A tender of rainbows must have a spirit of play and adventure. We will encounter surprises and unexpected turns. For when imaginations come to life, people begin to make their own connections and juxtapositions. Together, we may arrive at strange new places.

In one sense this whole book is a manual on how to tend the inner rainbow, how to nurture the link between faith and the imagination. Our focus throughout has been the pastoral dimensions of the recovery of the imagination. In this final chapter we will look at three additional ways in which a minister can foster the role of the imagination in faith: (1) helping people tell their stories; (2) learning to listen with the imagination; (3) being a witness of paradox.

Helping People Tell Their Stories

In a sense, telling our story is one of the easiest and most natural things we do. It needs no complicated formula or set of directions. We do it spontaneously. Yet a story demands a listener. What we most need is someone to listen to our story and help us to appreciate it in the light of faith. We see in the ministry of Jesus that he is not only a skillful storyteller; he also knows how to listen to the stories of others and help them to understand what God is doing in their lives. He challenges them to move further with their stories, to live out the call that is found within them. The New Testament shows us Nicodemus coming to visit Jesus at night (Jn 3:1–21), Jesus' conversation with the Samaritan woman at the well (Jn 4:1–42), and Jesus' encounter with the rich young man who recognizes his reluctance to follow him any further (Lk 18:18–23). In Luke 7:36–50 Jesus hears and understands the silent story, acted in gesture, of the woman who was a sinner. All these people found in Jesus someone who was able to tend the inner rainbow, to hear their stories and understand the unexpressed questions and yearnings they contained.

In order to listen to a story in this way we must believe in the uniqueness and importance of each story, of each individual's life before God. Most people are afraid to tell their story because they think that it is neither clever nor beautiful. No one would want to hear it. This shows how vital the openhearted, interested listener is.

The film "Peege" shows how redemptive it is to find someone who can hear our story. A suburban family visits the father's elderly mother in a nursing home. It is Christmas day. Through flashbacks we see Peege, now in the nursing home, in earlier times. She is a woman filled with life and vitality as she dances with her grandchildren and presides over birthday parties and summers at her cabin where they stay up late watching horror movies. Now Peege is blind and in a wheelchair, able to communicate with only an occasional word. The family tries to maintain an outward cheerfulness during the visit, though they are obviously saddened and somewhat repulsed by her racking cough and the catheter tube at her leg. They talk about people Peege does not know and about Christmas decorations she cannot see, and they give her presents that she does not want.

Without ever getting close to Peege, the family says goodbye and goes out to the car. Only the eldest, college-age son stays behind. He puts his arm around her, his cheek close to hers, and together they tell her story. They recall memories which give her back her identity and link their lives. For the first time in the visit, Peege smiles. The grandson has tended the inner rainbow; he has ministered.

"Peege" brings out another aspect of helping people tell their stories. In the movie we see that imagination is a relational activity. We imagine best when we are with others. Sometimes we cannot imagine anything new at all when we are alone. One aspect of Christian ministry is this imagining with others. It not only stimulates their imagination. Their sharing the fruits of their own creativity deepens the impression of it on themselves. We are support and guide as they discover their self-images or use their imaginations in prayer or inner healing. As William Lynch says well in *Images of Hope:*

> We are so habituated to conceiving of the imagination as a private act of the human spirit that we now find it almost impossible to conceive of a common act of *imagining with.* But what happens in despair is that the private imagination, of which we are so enamored, reaches the point of the end of inward resource and must put on the imagination of another if it is to find a way out.[1]

Lynch equates the life of hope with the life of the imagination. Both hope and imagination rely on mutuality. When we imagine with others, we create hope in one another. This is what a community of Christians is meant to do.

This mutual creation of hope is especially crucial at present. As individuals we find it difficult to keep alive hopeful images of the future or to tell a story that has a future. We despair when we think of the problems of world hunger and nuclear war. It is only when we come together in a community that we can begin to imagine together a way out. We build hope in one another by revitalizing our imaginations, by dreaming dreams and nurturing light in the darkness. In Christ, sin, death and evil have been overcome. Christians are to be the edge of the future; they must therefore sustain a story with a hopeful ending. The minister is the catalyst and guide for this common imagination. He or she opens up new avenues of imagination by helping a community envision what cannot yet be seen: creative ways of solving racial conflict, a world without weapons and war, possibilities for sharing the earth's resources. The minister suggests to a community that the boundaries of the possible are wider than they seem.

Where does the minister obtain such hopeful assurance? In the treasure house of the community's traditions. It is the role of the minister to bring these traditions to life again so that they can call the community to conversion and comfort. In Luke's account of the first Eucharist, Jesus asks the disciples to repeat this ritual meal in remembrance of him until he comes again. The Eucharist is directed toward the future but rooted in a past event. The same is true of the Christian story which the Eucharistic ritual enacts. We remember the story, but in terms of dynamic analogy with our own life.

This is the way that the prophets ministered to Israel. In the hands of Hosea and Isaiah, the stories of Israel's past, the wilderness and Davidic traditions, are reshaped in fresh ways. They meet Israel's present story as sources of conversion and comfort. Hosea reminds Israel of her early history when she was open to God's love (Hos 11:4) and then uses these recollections to show the enormity of her present faithlessness and ingratitude. Isaiah remembers that God had established the Davidic monarchy for the salvation of his people. In light of this he points out the betrayal of Judah's leaders who refuse to vindicate the cause of widow and orphan and grind the face of the needy. Memory of the past also opens up a hopeful future: "I will make rivers well up on barren heights, and fountains in the midst of valleys, turn the wilderness into a lake, and dry ground into waterspring" (Is 41:18). It is imagination which enables these memories to live on in power. It taps their relevance for our present individual and communal stories.

Such living memory is the most basic meaning of tradition. Tradition is not a collection of past facts and dogmas; it is a series of stories which continue both to illumine and to shape the fundamental meaning of our present story. Tradition is the living memory which instructs and interprets our experience.

Latin American liberation theology takes the exodus from Egypt and sees in it the paradigm for the present struggle to win deliverance from oppressive overlords. Helping Christians remember and tell their story here becomes action for liberation.

In the example of Israel's prophets and in current Latin American experience it is clear how central certain paradigmatic events are for interpreting our stories. A paradigm is an experience which illumines all other experience, in the light of which its deeper dimensions are revealed. Paradigmatic events, such as the exodus, the exile, and the death/resurrection of Jesus, provide a lens through which we can view all the events of human life. Our access to these events is through the master images by which they become living tradition.[2] Jesus' ministry is marked by the use of such images: the Son of Man, the kingdom of God, the new Jerusalem, the covenant. By means of such images Jesus' disciples came to understand the significance of his life and ministry, as well as his relationship to their historical hopes. Master images span the distance which exists between our lives and the longer story of which they are a part. By seeing our lives as a covenant with God and with one another we link them to the stories of Abraham, Moses, Jeremiah, and the early Christians. We can then begin to view them in terms of God's faithfulness and our own response to that loving fidelity. In this way we respond to the questions of faith: Can I accept The Story? Can I participate in The Story? Can I come to see that it is really my story?

Through the use of master images, the minister can help a community to see that their many stories are in a sense one story. Images such as kingdom and covenant are relational. They span the distance between persons and enable each to share in the common tradition. The diversity and richness of each individual life experience remains; each of our passovers bears our personal stamp. At the same time, they all relate to the paradigmatic event of Jesus' death and resurrection. Through the use of master images, a common imagination develops which can be celebrated in ritual and proclaimed in story. It is this common imagination which is the measure of a community's unity. As a steward of the tradition, the Christian minister is architect of such a common imagination.

Another characteristic of master images makes them essential to our common storytelling. Since their purpose is to bring the light of revelation to our present experience, paradigmatic events and the images to which they give rise are like a new lens. It is not so much the images themselves which we know. Rather, we know our life in a new way through them. Ray L. Hart makes this point with reference to the prophet Hosea's use of the covenant image.

> Vibrant with current language, the image allowed the Israelites to see their existence as a whoring profligance and a denial of conjugal vows made with Jahweh and the earth he had given into their care. It is not Covenant but the violated earth and its frenzied social order that is "known," and known precisely in the presence of Jahweh the faithful partner to Covenant.[3]

As Hart notes, it is the prophet's gift of dynamic analogy, the imaginative linking of image to current situation, which is the basis of the image's power. If a minister deals in these images without relating them to our individual and common stories, they become dead forms known only for their own sake. The point is not to fix the mind upon the image itself, not simply to define covenant and give its historical forms, but to present the master image as a way of seeing our world anew. To accomplish this, a minister must tie the image to the language of our lives and our historical period.

A striking example of the way in which such a symbolic equation between image and current situation can minister to a nation in crisis is Abraham Lincoln's Gettysburg Address. Early America had few forms of public expression capable of communicating deeply imaginative symbolism. Public oratory, infused with biblical imagery, was one such form. In his address, Lincoln insistently uses the themes of death, sacrifice, and rebirth, as when he refers to "those who here gave their lives, that that nation might live." He resolves "that these dead shall not have died in vain; that this nation, under God, shall have a new birth of freedom." In a way that transcends the Christian Church, the Christian sacrificial event of death and rebirth becomes a part of American life as challenge and hope.[4] The image is not itself the truth, but the bearer of truths. It inserts our story and the history of our period into a larger time. In so doing, it calls us to conversion.

A first way, then, in which we as ministers tend the inner rainbow is by facilitating individual and communal storytelling. We accomplish this not so much by a set of rules or procedures as by belief in the sacredness of individual stories and in their capacity for creating a hopeful future, unifying the many stories with The One Story, and bringing conversion. The minister brings this potential to birth by making a vivid link between the master images of the tradition and present experience, enabling us to remember as a faithful community.

We mentioned earlier that a minister helps us to tell our stories by knowing how to listen with love. In the next section we will see that tending the rainbow requires that we learn to listen with the imagination in all other aspects of ministry as well.

Listening with the Imagination

We begin our ministry with the goal of bringing God into the lives of others. We soon discover that we find the God we want to give already there. Thus our ministry is transformed into an ongoing revelation to people of the God who abides with them. Then another thing can happen too. We begin to find ourselves ministered to by those for whom we care. In the midst of our desire to bring about change we learn that we must first be changed by those whom we want to help. To minister, then, we must learn to walk the path of contemplation, the way of creative receptivity. We must learn to hear the voice of God in the midst of simple human events: the cry of hungry children, the challenging questions of teenagers, the frightened faces of the elderly. But we must listen with our imaginations. For we saw earlier that it is the imagination which spans the distance between the concrete event and the universal presence of God.

When we have listened with our imaginations, we will not be tempted to bypass the ordinary lives of people in an effort to open them to the truths of faith. On the contrary, we will reverence and care for the human details of people's lives, for it is there that God's voice is heard. In working with married couples we will help them to see that it is in the struggle to resolve conflicts, to forgive when they have been hurt, to commit themselves to the process of growth in the marriage, that God is encountered and responded to. Faith is not something different from their efforts to love, a realm of prayer and church activity separate from their attempts to communicate more effectively with one another. The crucial contact with God is in the details of daily life. Likewise, in working with teenagers, we will not resent their awkward search for the meaning of person and freedom, with the mistakes and wrong turns it entails. Rather, we will hear, and help them to hear, God's call to life in this groping. As tenders of the inner rainbow, we strengthen the bridge between heaven and earth, between the details of our human lives and the gift of God's grace.

That classic of Christian ministry, Georges Bernanos' *The*

Diary of a Country Priest, makes this point vividly. This story of a young priest's work in a little French village is a story of courage and grace. But it is the courage and grace of things which are simple, ordinary, small. As the novel opens, the Curé looks out over his village, contemplating its boredom and loneliness.

> I thought of the cattle which I could hear coughing somewhere in the mist, and of the little lad on his way back from school clutching his satchel, who would soon be leading them over sodden fields to a warm sweet-smelling byre. . . . And my parish, my village seemed to be waiting too—without much hope after so many nights in the mud—for a master to follow towards some undreamed-of, improbable shelter.[5]

The novel describes the Curé's idealistic efforts to minister to the daily needs of his parish in ways that seem insignificant and ineffectual to him. It recounts his courageous struggle to love and to come to grips with his own weakness and the forces of human lethargy and cruelty. At the end of Bernanos' account, the Curé lies dying and a priest is unable to arrive in time to administer the last rites for him. We hear the Curé's final words: "Does it matter? Grace is everywhere. . . ."[6] The novel is a moving account of a minister who has tended the inner rainbow, finding God's grace in the midst of the small details of life.

Listening with the imagination also calls us to hear the truth in new ways. We usually hear most easily the truths which people share in clear, concise, and direct language. When they say "I have questions about God" or "I am afraid of dying," we can understand them. But people cannot express much of what they want to tell us in such direct language. As we have seen, the deepest truths can often be spoken only in symbol, myth, story, poem, or dance. A young chaplain working in a city hospital tells how he wanted to help a young child to talk about her terminal illness. He went into her room carrying a rose and a storybook and came out having heard her deepest fears and hopes about her impending death. The child could not share her feelings directly, but she could tell stories about seeds that die in order to become beautiful flowers, and she knew the sorrow a rose feels as its petals wither and fade.

A nurse working with a patient dying of cancer in a hospital remembers how the young woman told the nursing staff that she believed a beautiful orchid which had been transplanted could only bloom in peace if it were planted again in its original home. Finally, one of the nurses heard her message and asked if she would like to die at home. Another woman working as a minister in a hospice recalls how she had to break the news of their father's death to two young children. Then she spent the rest of the afternoon playing with them so that they could express some of their grief and confusion in the symbolic language most familiar to them. The point is that people may use indirect language to express their strongest feelings, questions, and convictions. We must be ready to listen when they write a poem, draw a picture, or share the truth in play, symbol, or story.

Sometimes our ministry requires us to call a community to conversion in its images. In speaking of images of women, we noted that the life of a community, as well as of individuals, may be constricted by the effects of an evil imagination. The destructive force of such images in our culture, as well as the redemptive effect of overcoming them, is beautifully conveyed in Ntozake Shange's choreopoem, *for colored girls who have considered suicide/when the rainbow is enuf.* Shange's poetry describes the experience of being a black woman in a world of deceit and loss. A collage of pieces by women in the colors of the rainbow, Lady in Brown, Yellow, Red, Green, Purple,

Blue and Orange, *for colored girls* is ultimately about the courage which overcomes such painful experiences. In the final poem, Lady in Purple describes what she and others have been missing as black women in America: "a layin on of hands, the holiness of myself released."[7] Destructive images must be replaced by others which are more adequate and truthful, because inadequate and distorted images block love and justice. The role of the aged in America is another example. At its most elemental level, the problem of agism is a problem of our images of the elderly. Attitudes toward the old are shaped by negative stereotypes. The poet Theodore Roethke sums up some of these dominant metaphors of uselessness and decline in his picture of an older woman.

> How can I rest in the days of my slowness,
> I've become a strange piece of flesh,
> Nervous and cold, bird-furtive whiskery
> With a cheek soft as a hound's ear.[8]

As ministers we must make people aware of images that support oppression and prejudice. We must challenge images that are destructive of groups such as the aging, minorities, and women.

These are some of the ways in which Christian ministry is imaginative listening: creative receptivity to God's grace in the details of existence, hearing the truth spoken indirectly, and being attuned to distorted images that weaken the life of the community. Such listening will move us as ministers into the paradox of existence. Let us look briefly at how this is so.

Being Witnesses of Paradox

We are all familiar with the image of the minister as a clown. Jesus' own ministry is the source and paradigm for all ministry within the Christian community, and there is a long history in art and literature of depicting Christ as clown. St. Paul says in his First Letter to the Corinthians that he preaches "a Christ who is the power and the wisdom of God. For God's foolishness is wiser than human wisdom, and God's weakness is stronger than human strength" (1:25). As the Dutch pastoral theologian Heije Faber has suggested, the clown appears to be the amateur amid experts. The clown's skills seem pitiable when compared with the great feats of other circus performers like the trapeze artist or magician.[9] Yet it is the clown who reveals the joy at the heart of the human condition. The clown is a symbol of hope, someone able to produce laughter, even though the clown is frequently a sad person whose life is no different from anyone else's. In the image of Christ, tenders of rainbows have much in common with clowns. They witness to the paradox at the heart of Christian existence: the mystery of death and resurrection. From the earliest to the latest New Testament writings there is a strange linking of words which we would ordinarily think it impossible to link: "rejoicing in suffering," "dying in order to live." The clown represents this divine wisdom in foolishness and divine strength in weakness. Why must we as ministers who nurture the life of the imagination enter into this same kind of paradox?

We have seen that imagination reaches life in its wholeness. But it is not a wholeness which is achieved at the expense of the individual elements. The beauty of the rainbow is its capacity to unify a variety of colors into a symbol of promise and hope. Only the imagination can put us in touch with the central paradox in Christianity, because it alone can unify dissimilar elements and hold opposites in life-giving tension. Christians who are challenged to believe in this paradox of death and resurrection, strength and weakness, service and power, must be able to tolerate ambiguity and mystery. Such acceptance of mystery is a condition for participating in symbol, ritual, parable, and story. However, it is difficult to see how such contrasts can be held in unity. Ministry must be a fostering of such symbolic consciousness.

The most important way in which we as ministers of Christ prepare people for entry into paradox is by embodying it in our own lives. Through our very persons, we open people's imaginations; we help them to experience life in its complexity and to see that greater beauty is possible in a unity of contrasts. How do we do this? We share our simple humanity, along with our belief in its greatness and grace. We relinquish a notion of power as hierarchical control and demonstrate a power of service which knows how both to give and to receive influence. We live out with our communities the parable of Jesus washing the feet of the disciples and asking if they understand what he is doing. We encourage others to develop their diversity and uniqueness without being defensive or insecure. We no longer approach the community as though we had no needs; we share the death and weakness which is at work in us and allow the community to minister to us too. We acknowledge that we are earthenware vessels carrying a treasure, that we are mixtures of doubt and faith, of emptiness and fullness, afraid of death and suffering yet willing to face them for the sake of greater life. Above all, we attempt to hold in unity in our lives that greatest of contrasts, the incompatibility between love and hate, by responding to injury with forgiveness.

We do not usually consider such elements of ministry to be matters of the imagination. But it is only the imagination which enables us to reach the heart of the Christian mystery. The deepest way in which we continue Christ's ministry is by embodying such imaginative truth in our own persons. Toward the end of his play *St. Joan*, George Bernard Shaw has Peter Cauchon, bishop of Beauvais, the judge who sent Joan to the stake, cry out: "Must then a Christ perish in every age to save those that have no imagination?"[10] As ministers concerned with the conversion of the Christian imagination, we must begin to answer this question with our own lives.

Notes

1. (New York: New American Library, 1965), p. 19.

2. See Ray L. Hart, *Unfinished Man and the Imagination* (New York: Herder & Herder, 1968), pp. 286ff.

3. *Unfinished Man and the Imagination,* pp. 304–305.

4. Robert Bellah, *Beyond Belief: Essays on Religion in a Post-Traditional World* (New York: Harper & Row, 1970), pp. 176–179.

5. Trans. Pamela Morris (New York: Doubleday & Co., 1954), pp. 1–2.

6. *The Diary of a Country Priest,* p. 233.

7. (New York: Macmillan Publishing Co., 1977), p. 66.

8. "Meditations of an Old Woman." In *The Collected Poems of Theodore Roethke* (New York: Doubleday, 1975), p. 151.

9. *Pastoral Care in the Modern Hospital* (Philadelphia: Westminster Press, 1971), pp. 81ff.

10. (Baltimore: Penguin Books, 1951), p. 154.